麦格希 中英双语阅读文库

成长的烦恼

第3辑

【美】弗瑞德 (Freed, K.) ●主编

王雨红　刘慧●译

麦格希中英双语阅读文库编委会●编

 全国百佳图书出版单位
吉林出版集团股份有限公司

图书在版编目（CIP）数据

成长的烦恼. 第3辑 / (美) 弗瑞德 (Freed,K.) 主编；麦格希中英双语阅读文库编委会编；王雨红, 刘慧译. -- 2版. -- 长春 : 吉林出版集团股份有限公司, 2018.3（2022.1重印）
（麦格希中英双语阅读文库）
ISBN 978-7-5581-4760-9

Ⅰ.①成… Ⅱ.①弗… ②麦… ③王… ④刘… Ⅲ.①英语—汉语—对照读物②故事—作品集—美国—现代 Ⅳ.①H319.4：I

中国版本图书馆CIP数据核字(2018)第046505号

成长的烦恼　第3辑

编：麦格希中英双语阅读文库编委会
插　画：齐　航　李延霞
责任编辑：欧阳鹏
封面设计：冯冯翼
开　　本：660mm×960mm　1/16
字　　数：214千字
印　　张：9.5
版　　次：2018年3月第2版
印　　次：2022年1月第2次印刷

出　　版：吉林出版集团股份有限公司
发　　行：吉林出版集团外语教育有限公司
地　　址：长春市福祉大路5788号龙腾国际大厦B座7层
　　　　　邮编：130011
电　　话：总编办：0431-81629929
　　　　　发行部：0431-81629927　0431-81629921(Fax)
印　　刷：北京一鑫印务有限责任公司

ISBN 978-7-5581-4760-9　　　定价：35.00元

前 言 *PREFACE*

英国思想家培根说过：阅读使人深刻。阅读的真正目的是获取信息，开拓视野和陶冶情操。从语言学习的角度来说，学习语言若没有大量阅读就如隔靴搔痒，因为阅读中的语言是最丰富、最灵活、最具表现力、最符合生活情景的，同时读物中的情节、故事引人入胜，进而能充分调动读者的阅读兴趣，培养读者的文学修养，至此，语言的学习水到渠成。

"麦格希中英双语阅读文库"在世界范围内选材，涉及科普、社会文化、文学名著、传奇故事、成长励志等多个系列，充分满足英语学习者课外阅读之所需，在阅读中学习英语、提高能力。

◎难度适中

本套图书充分照顾读者的英语学习阶段和水平，从读者的阅读兴趣出发，以难易适中的英语语言为立足点，选材精心、编排合理。

◎精品荟萃

本套图书注重经典阅读与实用阅读并举。既包含国内外脍炙人口、耳熟能详的美文，又包含科普、人文、故事、励志类等多学科的精彩文章。

◎功能实用

本套图书充分体现了双语阅读的功能和优势，充分考虑到读者课外阅读的方便，超出核心词表的词汇均出现在使其意义明显的语境之中，并标注释义。

鉴于编者水平有限，凡不周之处，谬误之处，皆欢迎批评教正。

我们真心地希望本套图书承载的文化知识和英语阅读的策略对提高读者的英语著作欣赏水平和英语运用能力有所裨益。

丛书编委会

Contents

1

The Hunting Trip

José *scurried* up a makeshift ladder, which was nothing more than strips of scrap wood nailed to the trunk of the ancient oak. He pulled himself onto the *flimsy* sheet of *plywood* that served as the floor of the tree stand. He gently set his rifle down and took a seat in one of the two *aluminum* folding chairs while his father slowly followed him.

狩猎之旅

何塞急匆匆地爬上一个临时凑合的梯子，这梯子只不过是把一些废旧的木条板钉在了老栎树上做成的。他把自己拖到了用薄薄的胶合板地板搭建成的树架上。他轻轻地放下来复枪，坐在了另外一把铝制折椅上，而他的父亲在后面慢慢地跟着。

scurry *v.* 碎步急跑
plywood *n.* 胶合板

flimsy *adj.* 轻薄的
aluminum *n.* 铝

José noticed that his father was slightly out of breath when he reached the top, stopping to pull a Thermos of *steaming* coffee from his deep jacket pocket and *grimacing* as he swallowed. José felt his own chest constricting and realized he had been holding his breath for some time. He recalled his father's advice about nerves—"deep breaths work better than you think"—and drew a big *lungful* of air. His father heard him *exhaling*.

"You nervous?" he asked.

"No... well, a little," José admitted.

"Just remember that we're the only ones out here for miles. I'd be the only one to see you if you did anything embarrassing, and I've

---

何塞注意到当他的父亲爬上树架时有点喘不过气来，便从他的深夹克口袋里拽出装着热咖啡的保温瓶，略带痛苦的表情开始大口大口地喝起来。何塞感到胸部收缩，这才意识到他已经屏住呼吸有段时间了。他回想起他的父亲关于紧张的建议——深呼吸比你想象的还管用——于是深深地大吸了一口气。他的父亲听到了他的吐息声。

于是问道："你紧张吗？"

"不……嗯，有那么一点儿。"何塞承认。

"只要记住这方圆几英里只有我们两个人。如果你做出什么尴尬的事情，我是唯一一个能看到的，而我已经看过你做了好多尴尬的事

---

steaming *adj.* 非常热的　　　　　　　grimace *v.* （因痛苦、厌恶等）扮怪相
lungful *n.* 一大口（一次吸入的空气、烟等）　　exhale *v.* 呼气

seen you do plenty of embarrassing things," his father chuckled.

"I know," José said. He took another deep breath, tasting the freshness of the woods around them, watching the *vapor* cloud *materialize* in front of his face. But he still *clutched* the barrel of his rifle so tightly that his fingers grew numb. He regretted being so anxious, unable to truly enjoy the beauty of the forest around them. The open *meadow* below the tree stand was dim and frosty on this early November morning.

"Now that we're set in our place, we'll need to wait quietly for about half an hour before the animals forget we're here. Until then, we probably won' t see a thing," José's father explained.

情了。"他的父亲轻声笑道。

"我知道。"何塞说。他又深吸了一口气，品味着周围树林散发的清新气味，注视着充满水气的薄雾在自己面前渐渐质化。但他仍然牢牢地握住来复枪管，以至于他的手指渐渐变得麻木。他很后悔自己如此焦虑，却没能真正地去欣赏周围森林的美景。在这个十一月初的早晨，树架下面的旷野草地是如此阴冷昏暗。

何塞的父亲讲解道："现在我们已经就位了。我们需要安安静静地等上半个小时，好让动物门忘记我们的存在。在那之前，我们可能看不到任何动物。"

vapor *n.* 蒸气；雾气　　　　　　　materialize *v.* 突然出现
clutch *v.* 紧握　　　　　　　　　meadow *n.* 草地

Remaining still for half an hour dragged on forever, and as his father had promised, they saw nothing. But just as the minute hand of José's watch seemed about to give up and freeze altogether, he heard a *rustle*—a squirrel. Soon he heard other creatures; crows and *ravens* flapped overhead, cawing and *croaking*, leaving José wondering whether the birds' breath also left little clouds in the air. Three or four rabbits browsed among the leaf litter underneath the tree stand. Suddenly José and his father heard the sharp footfalls of their approaching *quarry*—the white-tailed deer.

All the hunting advice José's father had ever given him began to rush through José's head: "Don't ever shoot unless you're absolutely

---

经过了度日如年般的半个小时，保持着一动不动，而就像他的父亲保证的那样，他们什么猎物也没看到。但正当何塞手表的分针似乎正要放弃运转完全冻结的时候，他听到了沙沙的声音——是一只小松鼠。一会儿，他又听到了其他动物的声响，乌鸦和渡鸦嘎嘎地尖叫着拍打着翅膀从他们头顶上飞过，只留下何塞在那里疑惑着，是不是鸟儿的呼吸也能在空气中留下些许哈气呢？树架下面的落叶中，三四只兔子在吃草。突然，何塞和他的父亲听到了正在不断接近中猎物的明显脚步声———头白尾鹿。

何塞父亲曾经给他的所有关于狩猎的建议开始在何塞的脑海里闪过："除非你确定看到了鹿角，否则一定不要开枪——我们不想射杀雌

---

rustle *n.* 沙沙声   raven *n.* 渡鸦

croak *v.* 呱呱叫   quarry *n.* 猎物

sure you see *antlers*—we don't want to kill a doe, and we certainly don't want to kill another hunter." "If you can't see more than half the deer's body at one time, you're too far away and there are too many trees and bushes between you and it." "Aim just ahead of where you want to hit, because deer move when you least expect them."

As if fulfilling a checklist in José's brain, a *buck* stepped smoothly into view. It definitely had antlers, it was in plain view, and José aimed his rifle just ahead of its chest. The buck was big and *sleek*, with soft brown eyes and a white *rump* under its flicking tail. José marked it in his crosshairs, feeling the trigger underneath his finger.

"José," his father said, not even whispering as he pointed his

鹿，当然我们也不想射杀其他的猎人。" "如果你不能看到大半个鹿身，那表示你和鹿之间的距离太远，而且有太多树和灌木丛挡在你们之间。" "瞄准你所要打的部位再往前一点的地方，因为鹿会在你最不经意的时候移动。"

仿佛是在何塞的脑海中核对清单一样。一只雄鹿缓缓地进入了视线。它肯定长着鹿角，视线良好，而何塞也用来复枪瞄准了猎物胸口前面一点的部位。这头雄鹿很壮而且皮毛亮泽，有着一双柔和褐色的眼睛，在它快速拂动的尾巴下面露出白色的尾臀。何塞通过瞄准镜的十字准线瞄准了它，触摸着他手指下的扳机。

"何塞！"他的父亲用他的下巴指着雄鹿的方向，用并不小的声音说

antler *n.* 鹿角
sleek *adj.* 光滑的；光亮的

buck *n.* 雄鹿
rump *n.* 臀部

chin toward the buck, "go ahead."

"No," José said out loud, lowering his *rifle*. The deer surely heard him, for it *swiveled* its ears around until all of its senses focused on the tree stand, *alert* and confused, before it jogged away.

"Are you angry with me?" José asked his father.

"No, José, I'm not. In fact, I did the very same thing the first time I went out hunting with my father."

José felt relieved. "Really?" he said.

"I have a lot of time to think when I'm out here alone in the tree stand, and I've decided something about hunting. When we buy meat at the supermarket, we never see the animal it comes from.

道，"开枪！"

"不！"何塞大声说道，并放下了来复枪。那只鹿一定是听到了他的声音，于是它转动它的耳朵，直到它所有的感官都聚焦于树架这里，充满了警觉和困惑，然后它慢慢地跑开了。

何塞问他的父亲："你生我的气了吗？"

"不，何塞，我没有。事实上，当我第一次和我的父亲出来打猎时我也做了同样的事。"

何塞感到些许宽慰。"真的吗？"他说。

"当我独自一人外出打猎来到这树架时，我有很多时间进行思考，而且我确定了一些关于打猎的事情。当我们在超市买肉的时候，我们不会看

---

chin *n.* 下巴

swivel *v.* 旋转

rifle *n.* 来复枪

alert *adj.* 警觉的

But when we hunt, we see the animal, and we shoot the animal, and we take it home and eat its meat. It's more than just eating—it's an interaction between one person and one animal. And sometimes the animal looks at you, and you know you shouldn't shoot it. Sometimes I feel proud to get a buck, like I've won a race or I'm a *cougar* that caught its *prey*. But sometimes I feel like you just felt, and I'm glad you have that sense, too. If you shoot even when your heart tells you not to, that means you're killing without caring, without paying attention to the interaction between you and the animal. Some people never shoot, and some people don't think hunting is right at all, and that's okay too."

到肉是从动物身上来的。但我们打猎的时候，我们能看到动物，然后我们射杀动物，接着带回家吃它的肉。这可不仅仅是在吃肉——这是一种人与动物之间的互动。而有的时候，动物看着你，你知道你不应该射杀它。有时我为我能猎到一头雄鹿而自豪，就像我赢得了一场比赛，或者感觉我是一头美洲狮，捕获到了它的猎物一样。但有时我的感受就像你刚才的感受一样，而我很高兴你也能有那种意识。如果你开枪了，虽然你的内心告诉你不要，那就意味着你只是在杀戮，没有同情心，没有注意到你与动物之间的互动。有些人从来没有开过枪，而有些人认为打猎根本就是不对的，那也没有关系。"

cougar n. 美洲狮   prey n. 猎物

José *inhaled* deeply and relaxed for the first time all morning. His father took out the Thermos again, popped the cup off the top, filled it, and handed it to José.

"You want me to drink coffee?" José asked.

"It's hot cocoa," his father answered. "I brought it for you."

何塞深深地吸了口气，整个早上第一次放松下来。他的父亲又拿出了保温瓶，"砰"的一声把杯子从瓶口上拿了下来，并倒满递给了何塞。

"你想让我喝咖啡吗？"何塞问道。

"这是热可可。"他的父亲回答道。"我特意为你准备的。"

---

inhale *v.* 吸入

2

Ricardo's Dilemma

Chapter 1

"**N**ow listen up, class. Don't forget to bring a *sack* lunch tomorrow for our field trip! We'll have such a wonderful time!" Mrs. Periwinkle called out.

Luckily, the end of the school day had finally arrived. The bell rang, and Ricardo was almost safely out the door when Mrs.

里卡多的窘迫

第一章

"**现**在全班都听好了。不要忘记为明天的校外考察旅行带一袋午餐！我们将会有度过一段非常美好的时光！"派瑞温克女士大声说道。

很幸运，上课日的结束时间终于到了。铃声响起，里卡多几乎安全地出了教室的门，但这时派瑞克温女士挡住了他的去路。"你是不是很期

---

sack *n.* 大口袋

Periiwinkle stopped him in his tracks. "Aren't you looking forward to our field trip for tomorrow? I am very excited for you to see the ballet and tour the Opera House. I know you'll just love it."

"Oh yeah, of course I'm excited. Thanks, Mrs. Periwinkle. I'll see you tomorrow." Ricardo forced a smile for his teacher as he walked quickly past her and into the hallway. The truth was, he was much more excited about the *playoff* soccer match against the Tigers, and the match was going to start in less than two hours. Ricardo was the leading *scorer* on his team, and the playoff game was all that his mind had been occupied with for several days. He reached the front door and headed outside. His fast-paced walk turned into an enthusiastic *sprint* as he pulled his cap tightly down over his head. "Look out, Tigers, here we come!" he shouted.

待明天的校外考察旅行呢？你能看到芭蕾舞剧和参观歌剧院，我感到很兴奋。我知道你会喜欢的。"

"哦，是的，我当然很兴奋。谢谢派瑞温克女士。明天见。"里卡多勉强为老师挤出笑容。然后经过她身边快速地走到走廊去了。事实上，相比而言，老虎队的足球季后赛让他觉得更兴奋，而在不到两个小时之后比赛就要开始了。里卡多是他们队的第一射手，这些天他满脑子想的都是这场季后赛。他到达前门，朝外面出发。他由快步伐的走变成了激情的冲刺，为了不让帽子被吹飞，他不得不紧紧地把帽子在头顶上压低。"留点神，老虎队，我来了！"他叫嚷着。

---

playoff *n.* 季后赛 　　　　scorer *n.* 得分手
sprint *n.* 全速疾跑；冲刺

Chapter 2

The following morning, Ricardo sat smiling as he remembered the winning goal he had scored at the playoff match. "I knew we would win!" he told his mother as she joined him at the breakfast table. "We're going to be the champions this year. I can feel it in my bones!"

"That's great, dear. Now, are you ready? We have to get going. I agreed to go on the field trip with you and your class since I have the day off work. I think it's wonderful that your teacher is taking you to see the ballet. *Cinderella* is such a fun story, and besides, not everyone has the opportunity to see all that's happening backstage before the show begins. This is going to be a *fabulous* day. I can feel it in my bones," she said with a *wink* of her eye.

第二章

第二天早上，回想着在季后赛上射进的制胜球，里卡多坐在那儿一直微笑。"我知道我们会赢！"当妈妈也坐到餐桌旁和他一起吃早饭的时候，他跟妈妈说："今年我们会成为冠军的。我能预感到。"

"非常棒，亲爱的。现在，你准备好了吗？我们得准备出发了。既然有工休日，我答应和你还有你的同学们一起去校外考察旅行。我认为你们老师带你们去看芭蕾舞剧真是太好了。《灰姑娘》是个非常有趣的故事，而且，不是每个人都有机会在演出开始前能看到在后台发生些什么。这将会是精彩的一天。我能预感到。"她眨了一下眼睛说。

fabulous *adj.* 极好的 wink *n.* 眨眼

Ricardo rolled his eyes, then grabbed his backpack and said, "Okay, let's get this over with." Little did he know that this *excursion* would change his life forever!

Chapter 3

As the class entered the Opera House, Mrs. Periwinkle gave their tickets to the man at the counter. He made a call on his tiny black walkie-talkie, and soon a tall, skinny man appeared. Max was his name, and he had rosy cheeks and an enormous smile that made it almost impossible for anyone not to like him. With an *exuberant* wave, he led the class to an *expansive* space where a variety of strangely dressed people were milling around.

里卡多不情愿地翻了翻眼睛，然后抓起他的背包说："好吧，让我们赶快把这事做完吧。"他一点儿也不知道，这次短途旅行将会永远地改变他的人生。

第三章

当全班都进了歌剧院，派瑞温克女士把他们的票交给了柜台的人。他用小小的黑色对讲机进行联系。不一会儿，一个高高瘦瘦的男人出现了。他叫麦克斯，他有着红润的双颊，带着巨大的微笑，让所有的人几乎都不可能不喜欢他。他向我们热情洋溢地挥着手，引导全班走进了一个到处是穿着各式各样奇装异服、四处走动的人们的开阔场地。

---

excursion *n.* 短途旅行　　　　　　　　exuberant *adj.* 热情洋溢的
expansive *adj.* 开阔的

The tour guide told the students that these were the stars of the ballet, which, Ricardo supposed, would explain why everyone was *meandering* around in tights and slippers. Some were *stretching* their long legs toward the *ceiling* while standing on one foot, and some were turning in circles again and again, arms stretched above their heads. Still others were sitting on the floor, their upper bodies bent incredibly far to one side while they rolled their ankles in circles. They seemed to be focused so intently on what they were doing that they didn't notice anyone around them. Ricardo watched, amazed by their concentration. He couldn't have imagined that ballet dancers were so serious about their work. "Just like a player warming up before a big game," he thought to himself.

Max led the class to the backstage area where all the scenery

---

导游告诉学生们这些是芭蕾舞明星，里卡多认为这能解释为什么每个人都穿着紧身衣和轻便舞鞋四处漫步。一些人正单腿站立将另外那条长长的腿向天花板伸展着，一些人在一圈一圈地旋转着，手臂在头顶上展开。还有一些人坐在地板上，他们一边扭转着脚踝，一边把上半身向一侧最远的地方不可思议地弯曲着。他们看起来是那么地心无旁骛，专心致志地做着他们的事，以至于没有注意到他们周围的人。里卡多注视着，吃惊于他们的专注。他想象不到芭蕾舞者们对他们的工作是如此严肃认真。"就像是在大型比赛前球员在做热身一样。"他心里暗想。

麦克斯引导全班来到后台区域，在那里所有舞台背景的各个部件都已经布置妥当，为演出做好了准备。那儿有色彩鲜艳的戏服，他还能听到管

---

meander v. 漫步

ceiling n. 天花板

stretch v. 伸展

pieces had been arranged and were now ready for the show. There were brightly colored costumes, and he could hear the orchestra warming up in the background. Everything looked so huge that it made Ricardo feel very small. The stage floor would soon be filled with the *twirling*, stretching bodies they had just seen in the studio. Ricardo felt the excitement grow even more as the *luminous* and colorful lights flashed on from the sides of the stage.

"Wow! This is really cool," he exclaimed to his mother. She smiled and said that she thought so, too. Quickly, he looked down and stopped smiling. He reminded himself that he was a boy who liked sports, not the ballet, and he looked around, wondering if any of the guys had noticed his enjoyment of the field trip.

"Still safe," he thought, assured that most everyone had been listening to Max. He heard Mrs. Periwinkle say that the show was

---

弦乐队在幕后已经开始作演出前的准备了。所有的东西看起来是如此巨大，让里卡多感觉自己非常渺小。这舞台上不久就会被他们刚才在练习场看到的旋转的、伸展的人们所充满。当舞台侧面明亮的绚丽多彩的灯光突然亮起，里卡多发觉他的兴奋愈发强烈了起来。

"哇！这真是太酷了！"他跟他妈妈惊叫着。她笑着说她也这样认为。顷刻间，他低下头收起了笑容。他提醒自己，他是个喜欢运动的男孩，而不是芭蕾，然后他四下张望，看看有没有人注意到他如此享受这次校外考察旅行。

在确定了大多数人都在听麦克斯讲话，他想："还好，没事。"他听派瑞温克女士说演出就要开始了。麦克斯领着他们从后台区域下楼，来到他们能看演出的地方。当所有人都坐在座位上以后，灯光开始渐渐暗了下

---

twirl *v.* 快速转动

luminous *adj.* 发光的

about to begin. Max led them from the backstage area and down the stairs to where they would watch the show. As everyone sat in their places, the lights *dimmed* and the orchestra began to play. Ricardo couldn't wait for the curtain to open.

Chapter 4

That night, Ricardo found it challenging to fall asleep as he lay in bed remembering the day. Mrs. Periwinkle was right—it was a cool field trip! He couldn't keep his eyes off the dancers. They were so strong, so athletic, so powerful and graceful. Was it possible to be all of those things at once? He remembered being so proud of his *heritage* when he saw the names of two Latino dancers. One was even named Ricardo. They seemed to enjoy themselves so much

---

来，管弦乐队开始演奏。里卡多已经迫不及待拉开帷幕了。

第四章

那天晚上，当他躺在床上回想着这一天，里卡多发现想要入睡非常具有挑战性。派瑞温克女士是对的——这真是一次很酷的校外考察旅行。他无法把目光从那些舞者身上移开。他们是如此强壮，如此灵敏，如此用力，又如此优雅。同时一起拥有这么多东西可能吗？他仍然记得当看到两位拉丁美洲舞者的名字时候，他是如此为他的民族传承而感到自豪。有一位舞者的名字甚至也叫里卡多。当他们在舞台上表演时是那么

---

dim *v.* （灯光）变昏暗

heritage *n.* 遗产

when they were on stage. At that moment, Ricardo decided that he wanted to learn more about ballet.

The next morning he shared his thoughts with his mother. "I think we should visit a dance studio and find out how much it would cost to take a few classes. That way, you could find out if you really like it or not," she said.

Ricardo really wanted to learn how to do all of the amazing things he saw the dancers perform. But what would his friends think? There weren't many boys who took ballet, and he was afraid his friends would *poke fun at* him. But Ricardo was self-confident. He was comfortable with himself, so he decided he would try a few classes. But he definitely did not want to share his plans with his pals. At least not yet.

Over the next few months, Ricardo took several lessons. His

享受。就在那一刻，里卡多决定他要更多地了解芭蕾舞。

第二天早上，他和妈妈说了他的想法。"我想我们应该参观一下舞蹈工作室，看看上几节舞蹈课要花多少钱。那样，你就会发现你是不是真的喜欢它了。"他妈妈说。

里卡多真的很想学他所看到的舞者们表演的所有那些令人惊奇的动作。但是他的朋友们会怎么想呢？可是没有几个男孩子去上芭蕾课的，他怕他的朋友们会取笑他。但是里卡多很自信，他对自己很满意，所以他决定先上几节课试试。但他是绝对不会和他的伙伴们分享他的计划的，至少现在不会。

在接下来的几个月，里卡多上了几节课。他对舞蹈的兴趣不断增长，

poke fun at 嘲弄

interest in dance began to grow, and his instructor told him that he was a natural. Playing sports had made him strong. His strength helped him perform new and difficult steps. He found that ballet was intense and challenging, but when he got something right, it made him feel like he was on top of the world. Little did he know that someday his dance skills would help him in ways he could not have imagined!

Chapter 5

One summer afternoon, Ricardo was wandering through the city zoo with his best friend, Zach. They had just finished a great soccer match—winning 5 to *zip*!

"Boy, it just seems like it's impossible for us to lose lately! Our

---

而且他的教练告诉他，他是一位天生的舞者。做运动让他很强壮。他的力量帮助他完成那些新的很难的舞步。他发现芭蕾舞是种剧烈的运动而且非常具有挑战性，但当他做对了一些动作时，他感觉幸福到了极点。他一点儿也不知道，某一天他的舞蹈技巧会以一种他无法想象的方式帮助他。

第五章

一个夏日午后，里卡多正在和他最好的朋友——扎克，逛城市动物园。他们刚刚比完一场重要的足球比赛——以五比零大胜。

"老兄，看起来最近让我们输球是不可能的了。今年我们的球队是我

---

zip *n.* 零

team this year is the best team I've ever been on. I don't want the season to ever end," Zach said. "Do you think our championship *trophy* will be silver or gold this year?"

"Definitely gold. And I hope it is six feet tall!" replied Ricardo. The boys laughed. They only had two more games to win to finish up the season as champions, and both were confident that they could pull it off.

Ricardo had been busy during the playoffs, but he managed to make it to ballet class three nights a week. It had become very important to him, and the better he got at it, the more he knew that he wanted to dance forever.

But Ricardo realized he couldn't keep his dancing a secret from his friends for much longer. He just hoped that they would somehow understand.

待过的最好的球队。我都不想让这个赛季结束了。"扎克说道:"你认为我们今年的冠军奖杯是金的还是银的?"

"绝对是金的,而且我希望它有六英尺高!"里卡多回答道。两个男孩大笑起来。他们只需要再赢两场就能以冠军身份结束赛季,而且他们两个都有信心能够圆满完成。

虽然里卡多季后赛期间一直都很忙,但他还是设法每星期用三个晚上上芭蕾课。这对他来说非常重要,随着他越跳越好,他越来越明白他要永远跳下去。

但里卡多也意识到,他不能再向他的朋友们隐瞒这件事了。他只希望朋友们可以理解他。

---

trophy *n.* 奖杯

Today, at the zoo, he had planned to break the news to Zach. He practiced what he was going to say a million times in his mind. He thought and thought. Finally, he came up with a list of reasons why someone would like to learn ballet. He practiced saying the reasons over in his mind. (1) There are men all around the world who dance ballet. (2) Some dancers are very famous and make a lot of money performing. (3) Ballet is great exercise. (4) There are lots of cute girls in dance class who want to be his friend.

Ricardo smiled as he remembered all the girls telling him that he was so cool for learning ballet. Surely the guys would understand at least that part of it. At least he hoped they would. He took a deep breath and got ready to spill his *guts* to his best friend. Just then the strangest thing happened, and it happened so quickly that Ricardo didn't have time to think—he just went into action.

今天在公园他打算向扎克说出实情。他在头脑中练习了上百万次要怎样说。他苦思冥想。终于，他想出了一系列关于为什么有人会学芭蕾的理由。他在脑海里练习说着理由。（1）世界上有很多男人跳芭蕾舞。（2）有些舞者很出名，而且通过演出挣了很多钱。（3）芭蕾是种很棒的锻炼。（4）舞蹈课上有很多想和他成为朋友的可爱女孩。

当他想起所有的女孩都跟他说他学习芭蕾很酷时，里卡多喜形于色。小伙子们至少能理解一部分原因的。至少希望他们能理解。他深吸了一口气，准备向他最好的朋友吐露心声。就在那时，最奇怪的事情发生了，而且它发生得如此之快，里卡多根本没有时间去考虑——他只是马上行动了起来。

---

guts *n.* 实质；核心

Chapter 6

Ricardo and Zach had just arrived at their favorite part of the zoo—the crocodile pond. They loved watching the enormous *reptiles*.

Ricardo had visited the zoo a lot, but he had never seen anything as crazy as what happened next. The boys were walking toward the croc pond when Ricardo noticed a baby girl *crawling* up onto the *teeter-totter*. Then from out of nowhere came this whirling, twirling, crazy kid. The kid suddenly jumped onto the raised end of the teeter-totter, not even noticing the baby! He was yelling over his shoulder to his friend, "Hey, dude! Get on!" As he jumped on one end, it *slammed* down and sent the other end flying upward. The infant was

第六章

　　里卡多和扎克刚刚到达动物园里他们最喜欢的地方——鳄鱼池。他们很喜欢看这些巨大的爬行动物。

　　里卡多游览过动物园多次，但他从来没有见过接下来发生得如此疯狂的事。两个男孩朝着鳄鱼池走去，这时里卡多注意到一个小女婴爬到了跷跷板上。这时不知从哪突然冒出来一个满地团团转的疯小孩。那小孩一下子跳上了跷跷板跷起的那一头，根本没有留意到那个小女婴。他转过头对着他的朋友叫喊着："嘿，老兄！来啊！"当他跳上跷跷板一端，这一端

reptile *n.* 爬行动物　　　　　　　　crawl *v.* 爬
teeter-totter *n.* 跷跷板　　　　　　slam *v.* 使劲一推

sent flying through the air, straight toward the crocodiles.

"Yikes!" yelled Ricardo as he *sprang into action*. Without even thinking, he put all of his ballet training to the test. He ran toward the pond as fast as his legs could carry him and leaped into the air in a marvelous grand split. Flying high through the air, he *snatched* up the baby. His fantastic leap and split was so fast and so high that it carried him over the pond. He looked down to see the hungry crocs with their large *jaws* wide open. He landed gracefully on the other side, holding the baby safely in his arms.

People all around clapped and cheered, "Hooray for the hero!" Ricardo couldn't believe it. A bulky man with *bushy* hair ran toward him as he held the baby tightly. "Thank you, thank you, my lad, for

---

砰地一下砸下来，而把另一端压得向上飞了起来。那个婴儿被抛到空中，直向鳄鱼群飞了过去。

"呀！"里卡多叫喊着一跃而起开始行动。不假思索地，他检验了所有的芭蕾训练成果。他以最快的速度拼命向鳄鱼池跑去，用了一个惊人的大劈腿跃向空中。在空中高高地飞翔着，他一把抓住了女婴。凭借他那不可思议的高并迅速的跳跃和劈腿，他越过了池塘。他向下看到饥饿的鳄鱼在那儿大大地张着巨颚。他安全地把那女婴抱在怀里，优美地在池塘另一边着陆。

周围的人们热烈地鼓掌欢呼着，"为英雄欢呼万岁！"里卡多简直不敢相信。一个有着浓密头发粗壮的男人朝着他跑过来，紧紧地抱住了女

---

spring into action　突然行动起来
jaw　*n.*　下颌

snatch　*v.*　一把抓起
bushy　*adj.*　浓密的

saving my baby's life," he cried. "How can I ever repay you? I insist on throwing a party in your honor. Tell all your family and friends to be sure to come. The whole city will be invited! No *expense* will be *spared*. I want to properly thank you, my hero!" Just as Ricardo thought things couldn't possibly get any more exciting, he heard someone calling the man with bushy hair "Mr. Mayor."

Had he actually saved the mayor's daughter from the hungry crocodiles? Well, that's what the newspapers said the next day. And that's what the newspeople from the television station said when they interviewed Ricardo. "How did you ever learn to leap so high

婴。"谢谢，谢谢你小伙子，谢谢你救了我孩子的命。"他哭道："我要怎样才能报答你呢？我坚持要为您举办一个派对。告诉所有你的家人和朋友一定要来。整个城市都会被邀请！不吝成本。我想要正式体面地感谢你，我的英雄！"正当里卡多觉得没有什么比这更让人兴奋的了，他听到有人向这个浓密头发的男人叫"市长先生。"

他真的从饥饿的鳄鱼口中救了市长的女儿吗？确实，第二天的报纸上是这么说的。在电视台的记者采访里卡多时也是这么说的。"你是如何学

expense *n.* 支出　　　　　　　　　　　　spare *v.* 不遗余力

and so *gracefully*?" they asked.

Ricardo looked straight into the camera and, speaking into the microphone, replied proudly, "Ballet! I love to dance." From that moment on, the secret was out. But he wasn't *embarrassed*. Instead, he was quite happy that he no longer had to keep his love of ballet a secret. And no one ever made fun of his love of dance.

会跳得那么高那么优雅的？"他们问。

　　里卡多直视着摄像机，对着麦克风自豪地回答："芭蕾！我喜欢跳舞。"从那一刻起，秘密就这样揭开了。但他不再尴尬，相反，他为不再需要为他热爱的芭蕾保守秘密而感到非常高兴。而且不会再有人拿他热爱舞蹈开玩笑了。

---

gracefully *adv.* 优雅地　　　　　　　　　embarrassed *adj.* 尴尬的

3

Losing Grandpa

Chapter 1   Where's Mom?

"What are you doing here?" Hannah asked as she walked up the front *path* to her house. Coming home from school, she saw her Mom's friend, Laura, standing at the door. Hannah's mom's car was gone. "Where's Mom? She's always here when I get home from school."

"Sweetie, something's happened. Why don't you put down your things and we'll talk."

失去爷爷

第一章　妈妈在哪里？

"你在这里做什么？"汉娜问道，此时她正走在通向她家前面的小路上。从学校回到家，她就看到了她妈妈的朋友——劳拉，站在房门的旁边。汉娜妈妈的车不见了。"妈妈在哪？每当我放学回来，她通常都会在这儿。"

"宝贝，出事儿了。你为什么不把东西先放下然后我们再谈。"

---

path *n.* 小路

Hannah rushed upstairs with her backpack and then hurried back downstairs. "What happened?"

Laura began. "Honey, your grandpa got very sick today and had to go to the hospital. your mom went him to find out what's wrong and stay with him for a while."

"What happened? Is he real sick? Is he going to stay at the hospital?" The questions *tumbled out* of Hannah's mouth.

"The doctors aren't sure what's wrong with him yet. Your mom promised she'd call soon after you got home from school and let us know if there's any news.

Hannah went to the kitchen to get some juice and a peanut butter cookie. As she *nibbled* on her cookie, she found herself staring into space. The house just didn't feel the same with Grandpa missing.

汉娜背着背包冲上了楼，然后又匆匆地回到楼下。"发生什么了？"

劳拉开始说："亲爱的，你爷爷今天病得很厉害，不得不去医院。你妈妈跟他一起去了并且要和他在那儿待上一阵子，看是否能清楚到底哪里出了问题。"

"发生什么了？他真的病了吗？他要住院吗？"这些问题从汉娜的嘴里脱口而出。

医生还不确定他哪里出了问题。你妈妈答应了你从学校回家不久，她就打电话，如果有什么消息会告诉我们的。

汉娜来到厨房拿些果汁和一块花生酱饼干。在她一点一点地吃饼干的时候，她发现自己正凝望发呆。缺少爷爷在的屋子感觉确实不一样。爷爷

---

tumble out 慌忙地出来   nibble v. 一点点咬

He had lived with Hannah and her mom ever since Hannah was two. That was eight years ago, and he was as much a part of her life as her mom was.

Hannah and her grandpa were good friends. When she was younger, he used to take her for walks around the neighborhood. He had to walk slowly because he had *arthritis* in his knees. Walking slowly was fine with Hannah because Grandpa had very long legs, and even with his arthritis she had trouble keeping up with him.

As they walked, Grandpa would make Hannah laugh by inventing silly stories about the people who lived in each of the houses. "Those people in that gray house over there, they have one hundred Bassett hounds. All day they take pictures of themselves with their dogs' ears draped around their heads." Hannah would *giggle*,

---

从她两岁的时候就和汉娜还有她妈妈一起生活了。已经过了八年，爷爷和妈妈一样都是她的一部分。

汉娜和她的爷爷是好朋友。当她还小的时候，爷爷就带着她在附近一带散步。因为他的膝盖有关节炎，所以不得不走得很慢很慢。但走得慢对汉娜来说却蛮好的，因为爷爷也有双很长的腿，即使是有关节炎，汉娜想要跟上他也很困难。

她们一边走，爷爷一边虚构一些关于生活在每一栋房子里人们的荒唐故事来逗汉娜笑。"那边灰色房子里的人，他们有一百条巴吉度猎犬。他们一天到晚用狗耳朵包着头给自己照相。"想象着人用长长的、油光发亮

---

arthritis *n.* 关节炎   giggle *v.* 咯咯地笑

imagining people with long, sleek dog ears for hair.

And that yellow house on the corner—the people who live there think they can fly. Every night after the sun goes down, they open their second-story windows, stand in the moonlight, twirl their arms, and *holler* for all the world to hear, 'We're getting ready to take off—just give us a moment to get our wings warmed up!'" Hannah thought Grandpa was the silliest person on Earth. And in truth, he probably was.

But the thing Hannah loved the most about her grandpa was how he made up different personalities for himself. One day he would be Il Baconi, the Italian *swashbuckler*. On another day, he would be Harry the Horrible, delighting in *zany*, ghoulish *pranks*. Each character had its own unique accent, and sometimes it like

---

的狗耳朵当头发，汉娜就会咯咯地笑出声来。

还有街角那栋黄色的房子——住在那里的人认为他们能飞。每天晚上太阳下山之后，他们就打开二楼的窗户，站在月光下，快速转动他们的胳膊，用全世界都能听到的声音高喊。"我们准备好起飞了——只要给我们一点时间预热我们的翅膀！"汉娜认为爷爷是这个世界上最荒唐的人。而事实上，他可能真的是。

但汉娜最喜欢爷爷做的事儿是如何把自己装扮成不同的人物。某一天他会是伊尔·巴科尼，那个意大利暴徒。改天他会是可怕的哈里，喜欢搞怪和骷骨类装扮。每个角色都有自己独特的说话腔调，有的时候就好像真

---

holler *v.* 叫喊

zany *adj.* 古怪的

swashbuckler *n.* 暴徒

prank *n.* 恶作剧；玩笑

the real Grandpa disappeared and the character *took over* completely. Hannah was never frightened by his *antics*—she knew he would eventually come back to himself, because he always did. Over the years, they did comedy acts that made them both roar with laughter. Hannah's mom didn't always understand what was so silly, but that never mattered, not to Hannah and her special buddy.

Chapter 2   Talking With Mom

Hannah was snapped back from her daydream by the sound of the phone ringing. "It's Mom! I know it is!" she shouted to Laura as she ran to answer the phone.

"Hello, Mom? Is that you?"

正的爷爷消失了。而完完全全地被所扮演的角色取而代之了。汉娜从来不会被他古怪的行为吓到——她知道最终爷爷会恢复到原来的样子，因为他总是会恢复。多年以来，他们做的喜剧表演都会让他俩捧腹大笑。汉娜的妈妈总是无法理解他们所做的荒唐事，但那并不重要，对汉娜和她的特殊伙伴来说不是。

第二章   和妈妈通话

电话铃的响声让汉娜从她的白日梦中一下醒过来。"是妈妈！我知道是她来的电话！"她边跟劳拉喊着，边跑去接电话。

"你好，妈妈？是你吗？"

---

take over 接管

antics *n.* 滑稽可笑的举止

"Yes, Hannah Banana, it's me," she heard her mom say. "Hannah Banana" had been her mom's special name for Hannah ever since her birth.

"What happened to Grandpa? Is he going to be okay?"

"Well, Banana, Grandpa got real sick this afternoon. He was walking to the bathroom when he suddenly fell down. He lost consciousness—that means I couldn't wake him up. I called 9-1-1. The *paramedics* came right away and took him to the hospital, and I went along. I asked Laura to stay there so you wouldn't come home to an empty house."

"But what's happening with Grandpa? Does he have to stay at the hospital?" Hannah asked impatiently.

Her mom began, with *hesitation*. "The doctors did some tests on

---

"是的，小香蕉汉娜，是我。"她听见妈妈说。"小香蕉汉娜"是从汉娜出生到现在她妈妈对汉娜的特殊称呼。

"爷爷怎么了？他没事吧？"

"好吧，小香蕉，爷爷今天下午得了很重的病。他在去浴室的时候突然摔倒了。他失去了意识——那意味着我没法去唤醒他。于是我打了9-1-1。医护人员马上赶来了，并把他送到了医院，我也跟着去了。我让劳拉留在那里，好让你回家看到的不是一栋房子。"

"但是爷爷到底出了什么事？他必须要住院吗？"汉娜焦急地问道。

犹豫了一会儿后她妈妈说："医生们给你爷爷做了一些测试，他们查

---

paramedic *n.* 护理人员　　　　　　　　　　　　　hesitation *n.* 犹豫

Grandpa, and they found out that he had a *stroke*. Do you know what that is?"

"I've heard of it before, but I don't really know what it is."

Hannah's mom continued, "The blood supply to Grandpa's brain got blocked, and his brain didn't get the oxygen it needed. Without oxygen, the brain gets damaged. That's a pretty serious thing, especially for an older person whose body takes longer to heal."

Hannah burst into tears. "Is Grandpa going to die? I don't want him to die!" she *blurted* out through her *sobs*.

Hannah's mom began to cry, too. "Sweetie, I don't want him to die either. We'll just have to hope for the best and send him lots of love."

明他患的是中风。你知道那是什么吗？"

"以前听说过，但我并不知道那到底是什么。"

汉娜的妈妈继续说：“供给爷爷脑部的血液阻塞了，大脑得不到所需要的氧气。没有氧气，大脑就会受损。那是相当严重的事，特别是对一个身体需要更长时间才能康复的老人来说。”

汉娜的眼泪夺眶而出。“爷爷要死了吗？我不想让他死！”她用呜咽的声音脱口而出。

汉娜的妈妈也开始哭了。“亲爱的，我也不想让他死啊。我们只能抱乐观的态度并给他带去更多的爱。”

---

stroke *n.* 中风   blurt *v.* 脱口而出
sob *n.* 啜泣（声）

"Okay," Hannah said quietly. "When will you be home, Mom?"

"I need to wait here at the hospital to talk with one of Grandpa's doctors. They're going to keep Grandpa here for a while, and I need to find out what their plans are for him. I don't think I'll be home until after you're in bed. Laura will give you dinner and help you with your homework. I'll see you in the morning. will you be okay?

"I guess so, Mom. I'm just sad. Sad and scared."

"I know, Banana. Me too. Here's a real big phone hung. Mmmmm! I'll see you soon."

Hannah hung up the phone and *flopped* in a chair. Laura tried to comfort her, but it was clear Hannah just wanted to be left alone. After a while she went up to her room and lay on her bed. She looked at the picture on her *nightstand* of Grandpa and herself

---

"好的。"汉娜轻声地说:"妈妈,你什么时候回家?"

"我需要和给爷爷治疗的一位医生谈谈,所以要在医院里等。他们暂时会把爷爷留在这儿,我也需要弄清楚他们为爷爷制订了什么治疗计划。我想直到你睡觉了我才能回家。劳拉会给你做晚饭并帮你辅导作业。早上我就会见到你了。你会好好的吧?"

"我想是吧,妈妈。我只是难过。又难过又害怕。"

"我知道,小香蕉。我也一样。给你一个大大的电话拥抱。嗯……我会很快见到你的。"

汉娜挂断了电话,一屁股坐到了椅子上。劳拉试着去安慰她,但很明显汉娜只想一个人待着。过了一会儿她上楼回到自己的房间,躺在床上。

---

flop *v.* 猛然坐下

nightstand *n.* 床头儿

feeding seagulls. Their time together at the beach the year before was one of her most special memories. She started crying when she thought of never getting to play with him again.

Hannah went over to her tank of *albino* clawed frogs and watched them *drift* lazily underwater. She had had many frogs over the years, and some of them had died. She knew about death when it came to pets, and she knew that people died as well. Her best friend's mom had died in a car accident two years earlier. Hannah had tried to help her friend with the sadness, but it was just too big. And the thought of losing Grandpa was so much bigger even than that.

Hannah decided to put away the thought. She ate a quick dinner of *leftover* pizza, did the little bit of math homework she had, and spent the rest of the evening watching television. She fell asleep on the couch, and Laura covered her with a blanket and let her sleep.

她看着床头柜上她和爷爷喂海鸥的照片，一年前他们一起在海滩的时光是她最特别的记忆。想到再也不能和爷爷一起玩儿了，汉娜哭了起来。

汉娜朝着装有白爪蛙的鱼缸走去，看着它们懒洋洋地在水中漂游。多年以来她养过许多白爪蛙，其中一些死掉了。当她的宠物们死掉的时候，她知道死亡的意义，而她知道人也是会死的。两年前，她最好的一个朋友的妈妈死于一场车祸。汉娜试着帮助她朋友从悲伤中摆脱出来，但那悲伤太沉重了。而一想到将要失去爷爷，甚至比那悲伤还要沉重得多。

汉娜决定打消掉头脑里的念头。她吃了剩比萨作为快速的晚餐，做了一点数学作业，用看电视消磨晚上剩余的时间。她在沙发上睡着了，劳拉为她盖上了毯子，就让她睡在那儿了。

---

albino *n.* 患白化病的人（或动物）

leftover *adj.* 吃剩的

drift *v.* 漂泊；漂流

Chapter 3　Morning Comes

The bright morning light hit Hannah's face just after 6 o'clock. She didn't need to be up yet, but the living room was much lighter than her bedroom, and she couldn't go back to sleep once the light awakened her. She drifted lazily in and out of sleep for ten minutes, and then she remembered: Grandpa's very sick, and Mom came home late last night. Hannah sat up suddenly and *darted* for her mom's bedroom.

Her mom was awake too, thinking about Grandpa. When Hannah peeked in the bedroom door, her mom said, "Come on in, Banana-girl. Why don't you crawl in bed with me for a little while and we'll have a little *snuggling* time?"

第三章　黎明来临

刚过六点，明亮的晨光就照在了汉娜的脸上。她还不需要起来，但客厅比她的卧室可亮多了，一旦被阳光弄醒她就再也无法入睡了。她懒洋洋地游弋在半梦半醒之间大约十分钟，随后记起：爷爷病得很重，而妈妈昨天很晚才回家。汉娜一下子坐了起来，冲向她妈妈的卧室。

她的妈妈也醒了，想着爷爷。当汉娜向卧室里偷看的时候，她妈妈说："进来吧，小香蕉女孩。为什么你不爬到床上来和我躺一会儿，这样我们就有点时间依偎在一起了。"

---

dart　*v.* 飞奔；猛冲

snuggle　*v.* 依偎

That sounded really good to Hannah. She crawled in beside her mom and nestled into her mom's morning warmth. She *savored* a few moments of closeness with her mom before asking the question most on her mind. How's Grandpa doing?

"Well, sweetie, I'm afraid the news isn't so good. They did a lot of tests on him and determined that he had a pretty serious stroke. He's in a *coma* now, which is kind of like a very deep sleep. It's what sometimes happens when a person has been through something *traumatic*."

"Is he going to wake up?" Hannah asked hesitantly.

Her mom took her time in answering. She was torn between wanting to protect her daughter from suffering and wanting to help her daughter learn how to face difficult things in lfe *head-on*. Finally

---

汉娜觉得这主意很不错。她爬上床挨着妈妈，在她清晨温暖的体温中舒适地躺着。在问妈妈那些时刻放在心上的问题前，她又尽情享受了一会与妈妈的亲密时光。"爷爷好吗？"

"好吧，亲爱的，恐怕并不是什么好消息。他们为爷爷做了很多测试，确定他患了很严重的中风。他现在仍然昏迷不醒，有点像在沉睡一样。当人经历了某些创伤有时会发生这种现象。"

"他会醒过来吗？"汉娜迟疑地问道。

她的妈妈想了一会儿如何回答。是希望保护女儿不受煎熬还是帮助女儿直面面对生活中遇到的困难，她左右为难。最后她深深吸了口气说道：

---

savor *v.* 享受
traumatic *adj.* 创伤的

coma *n.* 昏迷
head-on *adv.* 迎面地

she took a deep breath and said, "The doctors don't know if he's going to wake up, but it doesn't look good." Tears began *spilling* down her cheers. When Hannah saw her mom crying, she felt more freedom to feel her own sadness. She held tight to her mom and let the sadness fill her up.

Hannah's mom held her close and let her cry for several minutes. When she sensed that Hannah was calmer, she said, "Hannah Banana, how about if you stay home from school today and we go to visit Grandpa in the hospital? Last night I told the doctor about how close you and Grandpa are, and he gave permission for you to come to the hospital with me. They usually don't allow children into the *intensive care* unit, but they made an *exception* for you. We can sit with Grandpa for a while and talk to him."

"医生们不知道他是否会醒过来，但看起来情况不太妙。"眼泪已从她的双颊流下。当汉娜看到妈妈在哭泣，觉得可以更心安理得地去感受她自己的悲痛了。她抱紧妈妈，让悲伤填满内心。

妈妈也紧紧地抱着汉娜，让她哭了几分钟。当她感觉汉娜镇静了一些后说道："小香蕉汉娜，如果今天你不去上学而我们去医院看爷爷，你认为怎么样？昨晚我还和医生说起你和爷爷是那么亲近，他还答应让你和我一起去医院呢。他们通常不允许小孩进到特护病房的，但他们为你破了个例。我们可以照看一会儿爷爷，并和他说说话。"

---

spill *v.* 溢出；涌出
exception *n.* 例外

intensive care 特别护理

"But he's in a coma—he won't be able to hear us."

"Well, a lot of doctors believe that some people in comas can hear what is said to them. And even if Grandpa can't hear with his ears, I'm sure he can hear with his heart. And I think it will be good for you and me, too. We can tell him how much we love him and talk about all the things we've enjoyed doing with him over the years. Maybe talking with him will help us feel closer to him."

"Does Grandpa look *scary*?"

"He pretty much just looks like he's sleeping. A little different, but he's still your wonderful Grandpa who loves you. So what do you say, should we have some breakfast and go to visit him?"

"Yeah, let's go to see him."

"但他仍然昏迷不醒呢——他也不能听见我们啊。"

"嗯，许多医生认为有些人处于昏迷中是能听到对他们说的话。尽管爷爷不能用他的耳朵听见，我确信他也能用他的心听见。而我认为那对你我也都有好处。我们可以告诉他我们有多爱他，还可以说些多年以来我们喜欢和他在一起做的事情。或许和他谈谈话会让我们感觉与他更亲近。"

"爷爷看起来吓人吗？"

"他看起来就像是在睡觉。稍微有点不同，但他仍然是爱你的好爷爷。你认为怎么样，我们吃了早饭去看他好吗？"

"好，让我们去看爷爷。"

---

scary *adj.* 吓人的

Chapter 4　To the Hospital

After a quick breakfast, Hannah and her mom got dressed and drove to the hospital. They asked at the front desk where to find Grandpa, and then took the elevator up to the eighth floor. Hannah had never been to a hospital before and didn't like the smell of medicine that seemed to fill the air. She *peeked* in a few rooms as they walked down the hall and saw patients hooked up to all sorts of machines, surrounded by people with worried looks on their faces. This made her even more eager to get to Grandpa's room fast.

When they got to Room 824, Hannah hesitated. She was afraid to see her beloved Grandpa so sick, yet she felt a strong *yearning* to

---

第四章　去医院

匆匆吃过早饭后，汉娜和妈妈穿好衣服，然后开车去了医院。她们询问前台在哪里能找到爷爷，然后乘电梯上到八楼。汉娜以前从没有来过医院而她也很不喜欢那似乎充满在空气中药物的味道。当他们沿着走廊走的时候，她偷偷地向几间病房内张望，看到病人身上连着各式各样的仪器，四周围满了脸上尽是焦虑表情的人们。这让她更迫切地想快点到爷爷的病房。

当她们到了824号病房，汉娜犹豫了。她很害怕看到她深爱着的爷爷

---

peek　*v.* 瞥见　　　　　　　　　　　　yearning　*n.* 向往；强烈愿望

be close to him. She held back for a moment, taking in the reality of him being in a coma, and then rushed to his side. "Is it okay to hold his hand, Mom?"

"Sure, sweetie. Just be careful that you don't *bump* any *tubes* or equipment."

Hannah took his big, square hand in hers and felt the familiar warmth that had given her such comfort for many years. "Hi, Grandpa," she whispered. "It's Hannah. I came to visit you and tell you that I love you and want you to get better."

Hannah's mom stood back, letting Hannah have private time with Grandpa. She was so grateful that the two of them had developed

---

病重的样子，但她也有一种想要接近他的强烈渴望。她犹豫了一会儿，接受着他昏迷不醒的现实，然后奔向了他的身边。"妈妈，可以握着他的手吗？"

"当然可以，亲爱的。只要注意别碰到任何管子或仪器。"

汉娜用她的手握住了爷爷那又大又方的手，感受着多年来让她觉得如此舒服的熟悉的温暖。"嗨，爷爷。"她低声说："我是汉娜。我来看你了，还要告诉你我爱你，并且希望你站起来。"

汉娜的妈妈靠后站着，好让汉娜和爷爷有些私人空间。他们两个发

---

bump *v.* 碰撞

tube *n.* 试管

such a close relationship. It had helped to make up for the fact that Hannah's dad had left soon after Hannah was born. After Grandpa came to live with them, their lives seemed to grow calmer with his presence.

"Hannah, do you want to tell Grandpa what you love about him?"

"Sure. Grandpa, I love your *fuzzy* white beard that you always insist is black. And I love all those people you pretend to be and the accents you make up, and the stories you invent about people you don't know. And you make the best *scrambled* eggs in the world. And I love how you can fix everything that gets broken. But my very favorite thing is when we go walking in the woods and you teach me

---

展到如此亲密的关系让她欣慰。这很大程度上帮着弥补了汉娜出生不久她的父亲就离开了这一事实。自从爷爷来和他们一起生活以后，由于他的存在，她们的生活看起来变得更加平静了。

"汉娜，你想不想告诉爷爷你爱他？"

"当然了。爷爷我爱你毛茸茸的白胡子，虽然你一直坚持是黑色的。我还爱你装扮成的所有那些人和你编造的语调，还有那些虚构的你不认识的人的故事。还有你做的世界上最好吃的炒鸡蛋。我爱你能修好任何坏掉的东西。但我最爱的是当我们走在树林里，你教给我的关于河流、鸟儿、

---

fuzzy *adj.* 毛茸茸的

scramble *v.* 炒（蛋）

about rivers and birds and flowers and stars and moons."

Tears came to Hannah's eyes as she remembered all the *wonderful* times she had had with Grandpa. "Please don't die. I love you so, so much."

She sat quietly for several moments, just holding his hand.

When Hannah was finished, she got up and aid, "Mom, why don't you talk to him now?" Hannah went around to the other side of the bed and held Grandpa's other hand while her mom talked to him. After a few moments, her mom got up and went to find Grandpa's doctor to ask some questions. While she was gone, Hannah sat holding and *stroking* Grandpa's hand. Even though he couldn't talk, just touching him was a comfort to Hannah. She knew she might not

---

花儿、星星和月亮的内容。"

当汉娜想起她和爷爷一起经历的美好时光时，不禁潸然泪下。"求求你不要死。我是那么那么爱你。"

她安安静静地坐了一会儿，就那样一直握着爷爷的手。

汉娜完事了以后，她起身说："妈妈，你和爷爷说会儿吧！"在妈妈和爷爷说话的时候，汉娜走到了床的另一边，握住了爷爷的另一只手。过了一会儿，她妈妈站了起来，去找爷爷的医生问些问题。她走了以后，汉娜坐在那里一直握着爷爷的手不停地拍打着。尽管他不能讲话，但就这样触摸着他也让汉娜感到安慰。她知道可能不会有更多的时间了，于是他就

---

wonderful *adj.* 美好的　　　　　　　　　　　　stroke *v.* 轻抚；抚摩

be able to for much longer, so she *soaked up* the time with him while she could.

When Hannah's mom returned, she said, "Okay, Banana, it's time for us to go. Say goodbye to Grandpa for now."

Hannah leaned over and kissed Grandpa on the *forehead*. "See you later, Il Baconi. Please get better. I love you."

Chapter 5　The Phone Call

Later that afternoon, Hannah and her mom were looking over the vegetables in their garden when the phone rang. Hannah's mom went inside to answer it. She was gone long enough that Hannah

---

沉浸在她能和爷爷待在一起的时间里了。

当汉娜妈妈回来后说："好了，小香蕉，是时候我们该走了。暂时先跟爷爷说再见吧。"

汉娜弯下身子，亲了亲爷爷的额头。"再见了，伊尔库茨克·巴科尼。请好起来吧。我爱你。"

第五章　电话

那天下午晚些时候，汉娜和她妈妈正在查看他们家花园里的蔬菜，电

---

soak up 沉浸于　　　　　　　　　　　　　　　forehead　*n.* 额头

began to wonder what was going on. She went inside and found her mom sitting on the couch with tears streaming down her face.

"That was a call from the hospital, Banana," Hannah's mom said through her tears. "Come here and sit with me, sweetie."

"What happened, Mom?" Hannah didn't want to hear, but she couldn't help but ask.

"Grandpa's heartbeat became *irregular* a little while ago, and some doctors and nurses rushed in to try to help him. They did everything they could ..." Hannah's mom *paused* to take a deep breath and calm herself for what came next. "But they couldn't save him. Grandpa died."

Hannah *burst into tears*, and the two of them just sat and cried for

---

话响了起来。汉娜的妈妈到里面去接电话。她去了好长时间，以至于汉娜开始怀疑发生了什么。她进到屋子里面发现妈妈坐在沙发上以泪洗面。

"那是医院来的电话，小香蕉。"汉娜的妈妈哭着说："过来和我坐在一起，亲爱的。"

"发生什么了，妈妈？"汉娜虽然不想听，但还是忍不住问。

"刚才爷爷的心跳变得很不规律，医生和护士们都拥上来设法救他。他们尽力了……"汉娜的妈妈停顿了一下，深吸一口气，让自己平静下来好说接下来的话。"但他们没能救得了他。爷爷去世了。"

汉娜放声痛哭起来，她们俩就坐在那儿哭了好久，相互紧紧地抱着。

---

irregular *adj.* 不规律的
burst into tears 突然哭了起来

pause *v.* 停顿

a long time, holding onto each other. Hannah wasn't thinking about anything—her mind just went, and her tears were a huge river *roaring* through her heart.

After a long time and many tears, Hannah's mom said, "I'm sure glad we got to see him this morning."

"Yeah, me too," Hannah said. "Do you think he could hear us talking to him?"

"Yes, Banana, I do. I don't know what happens to people after they die, but I do know that it's important for them to feel loved at the end of their lives. I'm sure that Grandpa felt deeply loved by both of us."

The next few days were a *whirlwind* of relatives and friends

---

汉娜什么都没想——她的大脑一片空白，眼睛就像一条大河从她心中咆哮而过。

过了很久，流了很多眼泪，汉娜的妈妈才说："我好庆幸早上我们去看了爷爷。"

"是啊，我也是。"汉娜说："你认为他会听到我们和他说的话吗？"

"会的，小香蕉，我相信他会听到的。我不知道人死了以后会发生什么，但我确实知道在他们生命的终点能感觉到被爱是多么重要。我确信爷爷感觉到了我们对他的深深的爱。"

接下来的几天里，亲戚朋友们像走马灯似的带着食物来陪伴汉娜和她

---

roar *v.* 咆哮

whirlwind *n.* 旋风

bringing food and keeping Hannah and her mom *company*. Laura stayed at their house most of the time, helping Hannah's mom make decisions about the *funeral* and just being there for comfort and support.

Hannah spent a lot of time in her room, drawing or talking to her frogs. She wanted to be alone much of the time, and her mom knew that was okay. She knew Hannah needed time to feel her feelings, and to not always be distracted from that. She trusted that Hannah would heal over time from this deep sadness, although there would always be an emptiness inside her from losing her sweet Grandpa.

When the time came for the funeral, Hannah didn't want to go. She didn't want to be reminded yet again that he had died. Her mom understood that Hannah was just very, very sad, but she

---

的妈妈。劳拉大多数时间都是待在他们家，帮助汉娜的妈妈决定一些关于葬礼的事，或者就是在那儿给予他们安慰和支持。

汉娜花了很长时间待在房间里画画或是和她的白爪蛙讲话。大部分时间她想一个人待着，而她妈妈知道那样挺好的。她知道汉娜需要时间去体会她的感受，而不想被过多地打扰。她相信汉娜总有一刻会从那巨大的悲伤中痊愈的，虽然失去她亲爱的爷爷终究会在她的内心留下空虚。

到了葬礼的时间，汉娜却不想参加。她还不想再次想起他已经去世了。她妈妈理解汉娜只是因为太过悲伤，但她知道让汉娜参加葬礼非常重要。葬礼对汉娜来说是一个和爷爷说再见的机会，也是体会被那些同样爱

---

company *v.* 陪伴

funeral *n.* 葬礼

knew that it was important for Hannah to go. The funeral was an *opportunity* for Hannah to say goodbye to him and to feel supported by other people who also had loved him.

Hannah snuggled up to her mom during the funeral and listened while many family members and friends took turns talking about what Grandpa had meant to them. Hannah never before thought about the rest of Grandpa's life—she had only thought about her felt a part of a great circle of people who all loved him, and she didn't feel so alone in her sadness.

Chapter 6　Starting to Heal

Two weeks after the funeral, Hannah and her mom went to a

着爷爷的人们支持的机会。

葬礼过程中，汉娜依偎在妈妈身旁，聆听着很多家庭成员和朋友们轮流说着爷爷对他们是多么重要。汉娜此前从来没有想过爷爷的其他生活——她只考虑过她和爷爷的关系。突然间，她感受到有这么一大群爱着爷爷的人们，而在她的悲伤中也不再感到孤独。

第六章 开始痊愈

　　葬礼后的两个星期，汉娜和妈妈去了家苗圃，并买了一株小日本枫

---

opportunity　*n.* 机会

plant nursery and bought a small Japanese *maple* tree, which had been Grandpa's favorite kind of tree. They decided to plant it in the back yard in a *spot* where they could see it from the window of the family room. While they were planting it, they talked about what a wonderful man Grandpa had been and how blessed they were to have so much special time with him.

After the tree was in the ground, Hannah petted it gently and said to her mom, "Now whenever I look at this tree, it'll remind me of Grandpa. It'll almost be like he's still with us."

Hannah's mom felt a warm *glow* inside. She knew in her heart that Grandpa would indeed always be with them. When you love someone deeply, the love stays with you forever.

树，就是爷爷曾经最爱的那种树。他们决定在后院能从家里房间能看到的地点把它栽下。在栽种小树的过程中，他们谈论起爷爷曾是一个多么好的人，而他们是多么幸运能和他一起度过如此特别的时光。

把小树栽到地里以后，汉娜轻轻地爱抚着它，然后对妈妈说："现在不论什么时候我看着这棵树，都会让我想起爷爷。几乎就像爷爷仍然和我们在一起。"

汉娜的妈妈觉得内心暖融融的。她知道在她心里爷爷将会真正地和他们永远在一起。当你深深地爱着某个人，爱将永远伴你左右。

---

maple *n.* 枫树　　　　　　　　　　　　　　spot *n.* 地点；场所
glow *n.* 喜悦；满足的心情

Leo the Lion

Leaving the City

The car ride was long and silent. Leo did not want to leave the city, but his father wanted him to meet his new girlfriend, Lucinda. The boy wished his parents were still together—that they hadn't divorced—but he felt *resigned* that there was nothing he could do about it. When he asked why his parents separated, his father would often say, "It wasn't in the stars."

狮子座

离开城市

坐在车里，旅途又长又沉默。利奥并不想离开城市，但是他的父亲想要他去见见他的新女友，露辛达。男孩希望他的父母仍然在一起——而没有离婚——但是对于这件事，他只能听天由命却无能为力。当他问为什么他的父母会分手，他的父亲总是会说："我们的星座不合。"

---

resigned *adj.* 顺从的

As they pulled off the highway, Leo noticed how different the scenery looked. Farmhouses and *silos* dotted the vast plains and *lush* fields. Herds of cows relaxed with their calves in the cool green grass.

As they ascended the hills, a *canopy* of trees covered them. It was so different from the concrete pathways, garbage-filled alleyways, and traffic-strained byways to which he was so accustomed.

"You know, Lucinda has a son in the fifth grade, too. His name is Dontrelle. I'm sure the two of you will get along just fine."

"I'm sure," Leo muttered *standoffishly* .

当他们驶离高速公路，利奥注意到景色看起来是多么不同了。农舍和谷仓呈罗棋布于辽阔的平原和郁郁葱葱的旷野上。牛群和它们的牛犊们一起在凉爽的绿色草地上悠闲地休息着。

当他们开上山的时候，树冠像华盖一样覆盖着它们，与那些他已经习以为常的混凝土道路、满是垃圾的小路，还有交通紧张的岔路相比起来，这里有着很大的不同。

"你知道吗，露辛达有个儿子也上五年级。他的名字叫唐催利。我相信你们一定会相处得很好。"

"我坚信。"利奥爱理不理地含糊着说。

---

silo *n.* 筒仓
canopy *n.* 遮篷

lush *adj.* 茂盛的
standoffishly *adv.* 冷淡地

Lucinda's house was *quaint*, *tucked* back from the road, bordering a forest. She sat on the *porch*, sipping iced tea from a glass with a slice of lemon clinging to the *rim*.

"Thomas, you made it." She smiled, skipping down the steps to greet them. Sweeping her arms to take in the view, she laughed, "Not quite like going to the office, huh?"

"It's amazing how different it is out here," Thomas agreed, greeting Lucinda with a grin. Then he put his arm around Leo's shoulder. "Lucinda, this is my son, Leo."

Lucinda extended her hand, but Leo didn't budge, keeping his eyes glued to the ground.

露辛达的房子古香古色的，隐藏在远离道路的地方，与一片森林相毗邻。她坐在前廊那儿，从一个杯沿上粘着一薄片柠檬的玻璃杯中，小口地喝着冰茶。

"托马斯，你成功了！"她笑着跳下台阶去迎接他们。挥动着她的胳膊好让我们看到，她笑道："和去办公室不太一样，是吧？"

"这里如此不同的景色真让人感到吃惊。"托马斯认为。咧嘴笑着和露辛达打招呼。他伸出手臂搂着利奥的肩膀。"露辛达，这是我的儿子，利奥。"

露辛达伸出手想和他握个手，但是利奥却丝毫没有挪动手的意思，眼睛一直盯着地面。

---

quaint *adj.* 古色古香的   tuck *v.* 把……藏入

porch *n.* 门廊；走廊   rim *n.* 边缘

"Sometimes he's a little shy," Thomas tried to explain.

Lucinda *crouched* down to Leo's height, which didn't require much effort because Leo was quite a bit taller than the average fifth grader.

"My son, Dontrelle, is around back. Why don't you hang out with him? I think he's about to go fishing? Do you like fishing?"

Leo didn't answer but *begrudgingly* dragged himself off the porch and toward the backyard.

Leo found Dontrelle pushing on a large tree trunk, barely managing to lift it off the ground. Dontrelle was much smaller and shorter than Leo.

"有时他有点害羞。"托马斯试着解释道。

露辛达蹲下来与利奥在同一高度上，这样做并不费劲儿，因为利奥比一般的五年级学生要高出许多。

"我的儿子，唐催利差不多回来了。你为什么不去和他一起玩儿呢？我想他正打算去钓鱼。你喜欢钓鱼吗？"

利奥没有回答，而是不情愿地强迫自己离开前廊，然后朝后院走去。

利奥发现唐催利在努力地推着一棵巨大的树干，但几乎没办法把它从地面掀开一丁点儿距离。唐催利要比利奥瘦小许多而且也矮了许多。

---

crouch *v.* 蹲　　　　　　　　　　　　begrudgingly *adv.* 不情愿地

"What are you doing?" asked Leo.

"A little help here," Dontrelle said, still *straining* to move the tree trunk.

Leo joined in, and with their combined strength the two overturned the tree trunk. Worms and *bugs*, now exposed, *slithered* around. Dontreele reached for an old soup can nearby and began *scooping* in fresh worms and dirt. Leo watched, narrowing his brow.

"Haven't you ever been fishing before?" Dontrelle asked.

"With worms? That's disgusting."

"What do you use?"

"你在干什么呢？"利奥问道。

"来帮我一把。"唐催利说着，依然在竭力地移动树干。

利奥加入进来，用他们的合力，两个人一起推倒了树干。各种蠕虫和爬虫都暴露了出来，遍地爬着。唐催利伸手够到放在附近的旧汤罐头盒，把新鲜的蠕虫和泥土舀进去。利奥皱着眉头看着。

"你以前钓过鱼吗？"唐催利问道。

"用蠕虫？那真恶心。"

"那你用什么钓鱼？"

---

strain *v.* 竭力
slither *v.* 滑行

bug *n.* 虫子
scoop *v.* 用勺舀

"Nothing. I've never been fishing.

I live in the city. There's nothing but *concrete* there."

"Oh."

Leo cracked a *faint* smile. He decided that Dontrelle was all right. The two exchanged names and handshakes, even though Dontrelle's hands were still covered with worm *slime*.

"My mom wanted me to take you fishing before dinner, but it's getting late, so we'll have to fish quickly. The sun is about to set. Grab those *poles* and let's get going."

Leo grabbed two long, skinny tree branches that each had a

"什么都不用，我从来没钓过鱼。

我生活在城市，那除了混凝土什么都没有。"

"哦。"

利奥咧嘴淡淡地笑着。他觉得唐催利这个人还不错。尽管他的手上还满是蠕虫的黏液，他们俩还是互相交换了名字并且握了手。

"我妈妈想要我在晚餐前带你去钓鱼，但是时候已经不早了，所以我们得快点儿钓了。太阳就要落山了。拿着那些渔竿，我们出发吧。"

利奥抓起两根长长的细树枝，每根上面绑着一条渔线和一个渔钩。当

---

concrete *n.* 混凝土

slime *n.* 黏液

faint *adj.* 暗淡的

pole *n.* 渔竿

fishing line and a hook tied onto it. When he looked over, he saw Dontrelle already on the trail, headed into the woods.

Into the Woods

The woods were *dense* and scented with musty dark pine, the kind of smell that clings to a sweater. Leo coughed as the cloudy scent *overwhelmed* his senses. He had a difficult time adjusting his eyes to the shadows in the *diminishing* light, and he tripped over a few *protruding* roots. Dontrelle paid little attention to Leo as he maintained a steady pace toward the creek.

A sudden rustling in the nearby trees made Leo jump. "What was

---

他再看过去的时候，唐催利已经朝着树林里走去了。

在树林里

树林很茂密，弥漫着发霉的黑松树的气味，那种味道能让人回想起一个大量出着汗的人。由于混浊的气味淹没了他的感官，利奥咳嗽着。一段时间里他很艰难地调整他的眼睛以适应逐渐变暗的光线下的阴影变化，还被凸出的桦树根绊倒了几次。唐催利几乎没有注意到利奥，还是一直保持着稳定的步伐朝小溪走去。

附近树林里突然发出的沙沙声吓了利奥一跳。"那是什么？"他尖叫道。

---

dense *adj.* 密集的
diminish *v.* 减少；缩减

overwhelm *v.* （感情或感觉）充溢
protrude *v.* 伸出

that?" he yelped.

"Nothing to worry about—probably just a *squirrel*," Dontrelle called back in an attempt to calm Leo's nerves.

It didn't work—Leo's breath became heavier and shorter with nervousness. Another noise only *exacerbated* his anxiety.

Leo darted, to the left, to the right, circling wide-eyed. "Is it a bear? Is it a bear?" he *huffed*.

Dontrelle stopped to look back. "There are no bears here." Just then a fox peered from around a tree, its eyes shining. "But there are foxes," Dontrelle added with a chuckle, pointing for Leo to see.

"没有什么好担心的——可能只是一只松鼠。"唐催利回头叫道，试图安抚利奥紧张的神经。

但没奏效——利奥的呼吸随着紧张情绪变得越来越沉重，越来越短促。另一个响声更加剧了他的焦虑。

利奥转动着因恐惧而睁大的眼睛，一会儿向左一会儿向右地猛冲。"是只熊吗？是只熊吗？"他气喘吁吁地说。

唐催利停下来向后看。"这里可没有熊。"就在那时一只狐狸在一棵树旁窥视着，它的眼睛闪耀着光芒。"但是有狐狸。"唐催利低声笑着补充说，为利奥指着方向好让他能看见。

---

squirrel *n.* 松鼠

huff *v.* 生气地说

exacerbate *v.* 使恶化

Leo screamed, dropped the fishing poles, and *bolted* farther into the woods.

"Wait!" Dontrelle shouted, dropping the container of worms as he chased after Leo.

After a while, Leo's *adrenaline* rush had *subsided*, and he doubled over in exhaustion. A *fatigued* Dontrelle finally caught up to him, and both of the boys tried to catch their breath.

"What's the matter with you?"

"I thought that fox was going to attack me," Leo gasped.

"Why would it like to do that? It's more afraid of you—especially

---

利奥惊叫着，丢掉了渔竿向树林的深处逃去。

"等等！"唐催利喊道，丢掉了装蠕虫的容器向利奥追赶而去。

过了好一会儿，利奥的肾上腺素激增终于平息了，而他感觉好像更加筋疲力尽。疲惫的唐催利终于赶上了他，两个男孩都努力试着恢复呼吸。

"你到底怎么回事儿？"

"我以为那狐狸要攻击我呢。"利奥气喘吁吁地说。

"为什么它要那么做？它更害怕你呢——特别是现在——另外，它那时好像离你有二十英尺远，正要路过那里呢，就像我们正好要路过小溪一样。"

---

bolt *v.* 逃跑

subside *v.* 平息

adrenaline *n.* 肾上腺素

fatigued *adj.* 疲惫的

now—and besides, it was, like, 20 feet away, just passing through, just like we were just passing through to the *creek*."

After a pause, Leo asked Dontrelle what had happened to the fishing equipment.

"Good question—I think you *ditched* it about a mile back, along with your bravery."

"Where are we?" Leo asked, trying to change the topic.

"Another outstanding question."

"Would you knock it off? How was I supposed to know that the fox wouldn't attack me? I've never seen a fox before—except for one time on TV; this hunter was hunting, and ... and ... and he got

---

片刻停顿之后，利奥问唐催利那些钓鱼装备的情形。

"真是个好问题——我想你把它连同你的勇敢一道丢在了后面，大概一英里远的地方。"

"我们在哪儿？"利奥问道，试着转变话题。

"又一个不同凡响的问题。"

"你可以打住了吧？我怎么会知道那狐狸不会攻击我？我以前从来没有见到过狐狸——除了在电视上见到过一只，一个猎人在打猎，而且……而且……他还被一只熊给咬了。"

---

creek *n.* 小溪   ditch *v.* 抛弃

mauled by a bear."

"A fox is not a bear."

"I know that!" Leo shouted, kicking some dirt in front of him.

"Okay, okay. Chill out."

"So, where are we now?"

"I don't know."

"What do you mean you 'don't know'?"

"I mean I haven't been this far out before, and with all of your *zigzags*, I lost track of where we were."

"Great. And it'll be *pitch black* out here any minute."

"That actually works in our favor. We'll be able to find our way

---

"狐狸不是熊。"

"我知道！"利奥大喊着，踢着他前面的泥土。

"好了，好了。冷静下来。"

"那么，我们现在在哪儿呢？"

"我不知道。"

"什么意思你'不知道'？"

"我的意思是我以前从来没到过这么远，而且随着你的曲折前进，我也不清楚我们在哪。"

"太棒了。这里马上就会漆黑一片了。"

"那其实对我们来说是有利的。在黑夜里我们能够更容易地找到回去

---

maul *v.* 袭击；撕咬
pitch black 漆黑的

zigzag *n.* 蜿蜒曲折

back more easily in the dark."

"What are you talking about? How can we get back when we can't see?"

"It's in the stars. Walk over to this clearing, look up, and you'll see."

The Stars

Leo looked up and saw a brilliant *array* of stars. His jaw *slackened*. It was quite a sight. He had never seen such a *dazzling* sky in the city. With the buildings and the streetlights and *smog*, that kind of view was impossible.

"Are the skies like this every night?" Leo asked.

的路。"

"你在说些什么啊？要是我们看不见怎么能回去？"

"星座会指引道路的。走到这片空地来，抬头看，你就明白了。"

星星

利奥抬头仰望，看到满天灿烂的繁星。他吃惊得下巴都松掉了。这可真是一大奇观啊。他在城市里从没见过如此绚烂的夜空。有着那么多建筑物、路灯，还有烟雾，是不可能看到这种景观的。

"每个夜晚天空都像这样吗？"利奥问道。

---

array *n.* 大量

dazzling *adj.* 灿烂的

slacken *v.* 放松

smog *n.* 烟雾

"Not on cloudy nights, but otherwise, yeah, it's like this."

The two boys gazed a little while longer, in awe, forgetting for a moment that they were lost. Finally, Leo asked, "So how are these stars supposed to help us?"

"Simple—by readining them. By reading the *constellations*," Dontrelle answered.

The what?" Leo asked, *incredulous*.

"The constellations—the figures and symbols in the sky that have helped people find their way for 6,000 years."

"Are you crazy? All I see are white dots."

"Dots?" Dontrelle was about to shake his head with disgust but

---

"多云的夜晚不是，但除此之外的夜晚，是的，都是这样。"

两个男孩又凝望了一会儿，肃然起敬，暂时忘记他们迷了路。最后利奥问道："那么这些星星该怎样帮助我们呢？"

"很简单——通过观察星星。也就是说通过观察星座。"唐催利回答道。

"星什么？"利奥表示怀疑地问道。

"星座——夜空中的图形和象征符号，六千年以来，它们帮助人类找到方向。"

"你疯了吗？我所看到的不过是些白色圆点儿。"

"圆点？"唐催利正要准备愤慨地摇头，转而却露出了顿悟的笑容。

---

constellation *n.* 星座　　　　　　　incredulous *adj.* 表示怀疑地

then smiled with an *insight*. "Yes, dots—exactly. All you need to do is to connect the dots and you'll be able to see a constellation. Want to try?"

Dontrelle pointed to a row of three stars in a *diagonal* row. He explained to Leo that by connecting the dots, he would see Orion's belt.

Dontrelle added, "The stars above the belt make up his chest, and the stars below it create his legs."

"No way."

"Orion was a great *warrior*. If you really use your imagination, you'll be able to see that above his head, he's holding a sword as if

---

"是的，圆点——完全正确。你所需要做的就是把这些圆点连接起来，然后你就能够看到星座了，想试试看吗？"

唐催利指着在一条斜线上的三颗星星。他向利奥解释着通过连续圆点，他就能看到猎户座的腰带。

唐催利补充道："腰带上方的星星组成了他的胸部，而它下方的星星构成他的腿。"

"不是吧。"

"猎户是一个伟大的战士。如果你真正运用你的想象力，你将能够看到在他的头上，他正举着一把利剑静静地等待着向野兽攻击呢。"

---

insight *n.* 深刻见解；洞察力　　　　　　　　　　diagonal *adj.* 斜的

warrior *n.* 勇士

he *poised* to attack a beast."

"Wow, I never learned any of this in school. I only learned that stars are far-away masses of burning gas, like the sun."

"Seriously?"

"Yeah, constellations are really cool, except I don't see how they'll help us get home," Leo muttered as he crossed his arms.

"As I was saying before, people have been using star patterns for thousands of years. Fishermen, that is, real fishermen, those who ride out to sea on a ship, not those who drop their fishing poles when they see a tiny fox—"

"Hey!"

"哇，在学校我从来没有学过这些东西。我只学到过星星是遥远的大量燃烧着的气体，就像太阳一样。"

"当真？"

"是啊，星座确实很酷，除此之外还看不出它们要怎样帮助我们回家。"利奥交叉双臂嘀咕着说。

"就像我之前说的那样，人类利用星星的形态已经上千年了。渔夫，我是说真正的渔夫，那些乘船出海的人们，而不是那些当看到一只小小的狐狸就丢掉渔竿的人……"

"嘿！"

---

poise *v.* 保持（某种姿势）

Dontrelle bit his lip to restrain his laughter. "Anyway, when fishermen were out to sea, they'd look to Polaris—the North Star—to *navigate* their ships because it was always in the north. Some farmers, even today, use Polaris's relationship to the horizon to determine when to plant their crops and when to harvest them. But if you can find the North Star, you'll pretty much never be lost. The North Star is always in the handle of the Little *Dipper*."

"The what?" asked Leo.

"Look." Dontrelle pointed up to the sky. "See the four stars that make a cup and then a *ladle* attached to it? That's the Big Dipper."

Once Leo spotted it, Dontrelle explained that the two stars on the

---

唐催利咬着嘴唇克制他的笑声。"总之，当渔夫出海的时候，他们却指望着北辰——也就是北极星——来为他们的船只导航，因为它总是位于正北方。有些农夫，甚至在现在，一直利用北极星与地平线关系来决定什么时候种植作物，什么时候收割庄稼。但是一旦你能找到北极星，你将几乎永远不会迷路。北极星总是在小北斗星的长柄上。"

"什么星？"利奥问道。

"看。"唐催利朝天空上指去。"看到那组成杯子状的四颗星星，还有附属着杯子的长柄了吗？那是北斗七星。"

当利奥一发现它，唐催利就解释着，在杯子末端上的那两颗星星与一

---

navigate *v.* 导航；航行

ladle *n.* 长柄勺

dipper *n.* 北斗七星

end of the cup were *aligned* with a bright star. That star, which begins the ladle of the Little Dipper, is Polaris, the North Star.

"So if we face that star," Leo wondered aloud, "we'll be facing north?"

Dontrelle nodded, and the two boys high-fived each other, *jubilant* that they had some hope of finding their way back in the dark. the celebration didn't last long, however.

Dontrelle's face grew sour as he realized hat knowing where north was didn't help. He confessed that he didn't know which direction they came from.

颗明亮的星星连成一条直线。那颗星，位于小北斗星长柄上的第一颗，是北宿，也就是北极星。

"所以如果我们面对那颗星星，"利奥说出内心的疑惑："我们就是面向北方了吗？"

唐催利点点头，两个男孩举手互相击掌，为他们有希望在黑夜里找到回去的路而感到兴高采烈。但是那庆祝并没有持续多长时间。

唐催利很失望，因为他意识到知道了北方在哪里并没有多大用处。他承认并不知道他们来的方向。

---

align *v.* 使成一直线

jubilant *adj.* 欢欣鼓舞的

"Don't worry," Leo said. "When we started out on our *expedition*, I noticed that the sun was setting in front of us. I don't see many sunsets back home, so it made an impression on me. My science teacher told us once that the sun always 'sets in the west,' which sort of rhymes, so I remembered it. When we left your house, we must have been walking west, toward the setting sun. To get back, we need to face north and walk east—to the right."

Relief washed over Dontrelle's face.

Leo continued, "I suspect that at some point we'll hit that creek of yours. If we follow it back, still heading east, we should come to your house, right?"

"别着急。"利奥说:"当开始我们的探险时,我注意到太阳是从我们的面前落下了。我在家那边很少见到日落,所以那给我留下了很深刻的印象。我的自然科学老师有一次告诉我们,太阳总是从西边落下。听起来有点押韵,所以我就记住了这句话。当我们离开你家的时候,一定是向西走的,朝着日落的方向。要回去,我们就需要面向北方,然后向东边走——也就是往右边走。"

唐催利的脸上洋溢着宽慰的表情。

利奥继续说道:"我猜想在某一时刻,我们会遇到你的那条小溪。如果我们沿着溪流继续朝东边往回走,我们就应该能走到你家了,对吗?"

---

expedition *n.* 远征

"You're a genius!"

Dontrelle and Leo were in high spirits. The two had helped each other with their *respective* knowledge. Both were excited to get back and, since it was long past dinnertime, they were both hungry. But their excitement was short-lived.

More Noises

After just a few minutes, the boys heard noises again. Leo panicked. Dontrelle tried to calm him down, but Leo was far too frightened. He began to breathe faster and dart around again. Knowing that Leo could bolt at any moment, delaying their arrival time even further, Dontrelle distracted him with the stars.

"你真是个天才！"

唐催利和利奥都情绪高涨。两个人用他们各自的知识互相帮助着。尽管晚餐已经过了很长时间，而且他们都已饥肠辘辘，但他们俩都为找到回去的路而感到激动。但他们的兴奋只是短暂的。

更多的声响

只过了几分钟，男孩们又听到了声响。利奥惊惶失措。唐催利试着安抚他，但利奥太害怕了。他的呼吸开始急促并且又到处乱跑起来。知道利奥随时可能逃跑，耽误他们更多的时间才能到家，唐催利用星座来使他分心。

---

respective *adj.* 各自的

"Did you know that there's a constellation named after you?"

"Stop it—I'm terrified that the fox is after me again."

"Seriously. 'Leo the Lion is a constellation."

The anxious fifth grader began to listen.

"Really?"

Dontrelle pointed toward the Big Dipper.

"Remember that star on the tip of the cup that pointed to the North Star? Find that same one, but instead look south. See that bright white star, the one that looks almost blue? That's right in the middle of Leo's chest. Some say it's his heart."

Leo followed Dontrelle's *gaze* into the heavens.

"你知道吗，有一个星座是用你的名字来命名的？"

"少来了——我很害怕又会有狐狸跟着我。"

"真的。雄师利奥是一个星座。"

这个焦虑的五年级小学生开始倾听。

"真的吗？"

唐催利指向北斗七星。

"还记得在杯子顶端指向北极星的那颗星星吗？找到同样那颗星星，但是要改为向南边看。看到那明亮的白星了吗，那颗看起来几乎是蓝色的星星了吗？那是狮子座胸部的正中心。有人说那是他的心脏。"

利奥随着唐催利的话凝望天空。

---

gaze *n.* 凝视

"Legend has it that Leo the Lion had the toughest skin of all the great animals. It was *impenetrable*, so he feared nothing."

Leo and Dontrelle stood in silence for a moment, regarding the lion in the sky. Finally, Leo felt he could be brave like the lion and nodded to Dontrelle that he was ready to continue.

The boys heard the creek before they saw it, but once they caught sight of it they ran to it, overjoyed. The two kicked water at each other and laughed. They had almost made it—now all they needed to do was to follow the creek home.

The boys *reoriented* themselves one last time before starting to hike again. But their eager steps were *suspended* in midair when they

---

"传说雄狮利奥在所有大型动物中有着最坚韧的外皮。无法刺透的，所以他无所畏惧。"

利奥和唐催利静静地站了一会儿，注视着夜空中的狮子座。终于，利奥觉得他能够像雄狮利奥一样勇敢了，他朝唐催利点了点头，表示他已经准备好继续上路了。

在看到小溪以前男孩们就已经听到了它的声音，但当他们一瞥见它就朝它跑了过去，高兴极了。两个人笑着，互相踢着水。他们就要成功了——现在他们需要做的只是顺着小溪回家了。

再次徒步出发之前，男孩们最后一次调整了方向。但当他们听到前方

---

impenetrable *adj.* 不能穿过的   reorient *v.* 使适应
suspend *v.* 悬浮

heard a noise up ahead.

The two froze and strained their ears. Sweat began to *bead* on Leo's forehead. Dontrelle held his breath. Then it came from behind the bushes—a fox, a mere five feet away.

Its long, bushy tail *flicked* back and forth. The fox *furtively* crept onto a rock in front of them and slowly craned its neck down toward the creek. Just before its tongue touched the crisp water, Leo shifted his weight onto his other foot, inadvertently *snapping* a twig.

The fox twisted its neck over in Leo's direction and locked eyes with him. No one moved— neither boy nor beast. Then Leo started

---

一个声音时，他们热切的脚步悬停在了半空中。

两个人都站住不动了，竖起耳朵仔细听。汗水在利奥的额头上形成水珠。唐催利屏住了呼吸。就在那时，一只狐狸从灌木丛后面出来了，离他们仅仅有五英尺远的距离。

它那长长的浓密的尾巴来回摇摆着。狐狸鬼鬼祟祟地爬上它们前面的一块岩石上，慢慢地朝着小溪伸长了脖子。就在它的舌头要碰到泛着波纹的水面之前利奥把他的重心转移到他的另一只脚上，一不小心啪的一声踩断了一根小树枝。

狐狸朝利奥的方向扭转它的脖子，并盯着他看。不论是男孩们还是那

---

bead *v.* 形成珠状

furtively *adv.* 偷偷地

flick *v.* 轻击

snap *v.* 弄断

walking toward the wild animal.

"What are you doing? Are you crazy?" Dontrelle *whispered* through his teeth.

"I'm just passing through," Leo whispered back.

"What? Why?" *stammered* Dontrelle.

"It's in the stars."

Leo slowly walked toward the fox. After just a few steps, the rust-colored animal bounded away, across the creek and into the woods.

Dontrelle exhaled.

"You are the fearless lion."

野兽都一动不动。接着利奥开始向那野兽走去。

"你在干什么呢？你疯了吗？"唐催利从牙缝中低声说道。

"我只是路过。"利奥低声回答道。

"什么？为什么？"唐催利结结巴巴地说。

"这是命中注定的。"

利奥慢慢地走向那只狐狸。只走了几步那褐色的动物就跳跃着穿过小溪，跑进了树林。

唐催利大呼了一口气。

"你真是无所畏惧的狮子啊。"

---

whisper *v.* 耳语   stammer *v.* 结结巴巴地说

"I suppose I am," chuckled Leo.

Back Home

When Dontrelle and Leo finally reached the house, their parents *scolded* them for their lateness but were relieved that they were safe. After a late dinner, Leo and his father prepared for their drive back to the city. Lucinda invited Leo to stay for the weekend, but instead he asked whether she and Dontrelle could visit them in the city. Lucinda promised they would. Leo extended his hand, and he and Dontrelle shook, knowing they would have many more adventures together.

"我想我的确是。"利奥轻笑着说。

回到家

唐催利和利奥终于到家之后，他们的父母因为他们回来晚了狠狠地责骂了他们，但同时也为他们安全回来而松了一口气。用过了迟来的晚餐，利奥和他的父亲准备开车回城里去。露辛达邀请利奥留下来过周末，但爸爸却反过来问她和唐催利是否能来城里拜访他们。露辛达答应了会来。利奥伸出手来和唐催利握了握手，知道他们将要一起经历更多的冒险了。

---

scold *v.* 责备

Horseshoes Aren't Just for Good Luck

Introduction

One of the best summers I can remember took place when I was just nine years old. I went to visit my great-grandmother. She lived in a big, old house at the *seashore*.

Leaving Home

Dad decided that this summer I should spend time with his grandmother, whom he called Gram. He said he had loved visiting

---

马掌不仅仅意味着好运

序言

我所能记得的过的最好的一个夏天是在我九岁那年。那年我去拜访我的曾祖母。她住在海滨一个大大的老房子里。

离开家乡

爸爸决定今年夏天要我陪他的奶奶一起度过，爸爸叫她祖母。他说他小的时候，很喜欢在夏天去拜访祖母。他带我坐计程车去了火车站。我一

---

seashore *n.* 海边

her during the summers when he was a kid. He took me to the train station in a taxi. I had always lived in the busy, noisy city. I was feeling a bit afraid.

Riding on a train, for more than an hour, was a new experience. The seats were huge and soft. It took *awhile* to become used to the rocking *motion* as the train moved south, taking me farther from home.

At the train station, Gram and her friend, Jim, met me. Jim helped carry my suitcases to his car. We headed to Gram's home by the sea. When we were getting close, Jim told me to breathe deeply so I could smell the ocean. It did smell different here.

直住在繁忙喧闹的城市。对于去别的地方我感到有一点害怕。

坐在火车上，过了一个多小时，我有了一种全新的体验。座位既宽大又柔软。我花了好长时间习惯了车厢的摇晃，火车向南行驶，载着我离家乡越来越远。

祖母和她的朋友吉姆来火车站接我。吉姆帮我把手提箱搬到他车上。我们朝着祖母海边的房子驶去。当我们快到那里的时候，吉姆告诉我深吸一口气，这样我就能嗅到大海的味道了。 这里大海的味道闻起来确实不一样。

---

awhile *n.* 片刻

motion *n.* 移动

Life by the Sea

Gram lived in a small beach town. Some of the houses were painted with many colors. There were not many cars. People were walking or riding bicycles. I saw horse-drawn carriages. It was so quiet. What would I do all day?

Jim said that he liked going to the beach very early in the morning to see what was left on the shore—gifts from the *tide*, he called them. I knew I had a lot to learn.

Gram's house looked huge and mostly gray. There were many flowers in the yard and we had to go up a lot of steps to get to the porch. Gram told me to look all over the house while she cooked

---

海边的生活

祖母生活在一个小海滨城镇。一些房子被涂得五颜六色的。这儿没有多少汽车，人们基本上是步行或者骑自行车。我甚至还见到了四轮马车。这里非常安静。我整天要怎么打发日子呢？

吉姆说他喜欢在天将亮的时候就去海滩，看看沙滩上留下了什么东西——他称这些东西是潮汐带来的礼物。我知道我还有很多要学的。

祖母的房子看上去很大，基本上是灰色的。庭院里有很多花，我们向上走了好多级台阶才到达门廊。祖母告诉我在她做晚饭期间，我可以在家

---

tide *n.* 潮汐

dinner. She said I could choose my bedroom from the three upstairs, but that my dad had always stayed in the one that faced the ocean.

The steps *creaked* as I climbed the stairs. There were three rooms, a bathroom, a closet, and a *steeper* stairway that went up to another floor. The three bedrooms had different colored wallpaper and lace curtains. Did I want green, yellow, or peach? Did I want to look into the neighbor's garden or out onto the street? As soon as I looked out of the window in the yellow room, I knew it was my room! I could see sand and birds and blue sky and so many waves.

My Summer Home

I *plopped* onto the high creaky bed and stretched my arms and legs. It was a long way up to the ceiling—much farther away than

里到处看看。她说我可以在楼上三个房间里选一个作为我的卧室，但是我爸爸一直是待在那个面对大海的房间。

当我爬上楼梯的时候，台阶不停地吱吱嘎嘎响。那儿有三个房间，一个盥洗室，一个壁橱，和一个通向另外一屋的陡峭楼梯。三个卧室有着不同颜色的墙纸和花边窗帘。我是要绿色的，黄色的，还是桃红色的呢？当我一从黄色房间的窗户向外望去，我就知道这是我的房间了。我能看到沙滩，飞鸟，蓝天，还有层层的海浪。

我的夏日寓所

我扑通一声躺到了嘎吱作响的高脚床上，伸展我的胳膊和腿。那是个长长的到达极限的懒腰——比在家伸的懒腰远多了。和城市比起来，这

creak *v.* 嘎吱作响　　　　　　　　　　　　　steep *adj.* 陡峭的
plop *v.* 扑通落下

the one at home. It was so quiet compared to the city—no horns, no *sirens*, no yelling. But as I lay there, I could hear the same sound over and over again. It was the sound of the waves, and I could smell the ocean. I didn't know the ocean made sounds—I had to get close to it.

I ran downstairs and told Gram I was going to the beach. She stopped me and said I needed to learn the rules of the sea before I could go alone. She put our dinner in the oven to keep it warm. We took off our shoes. The warm sand felt rough and kind of *tickled* my toes.

Gram showed me how far I was allowed to walk up and down the shore between two *jetties*. These jetties were walls of rocks built into

---

里安静了许多——没有汽车喇叭声，没有警报的笛声，也没有叫喊声。当我躺在那里，只能不断地听到同一种声音，那是海浪的声音。而我也能闻到大海的味道。我不知道大海还能发出声音——我一定要靠大海近点儿才行。

我跑下楼告诉祖母我要去海滩。她阻止了我并且说在我能独自去海滩之前我需要学会大海的法则。她把我们的晚餐放入烤箱保温。我们一起脱下鞋子。暖暖的沙滩让人感觉有些粗糙，让我的脚趾头有些痒痒的。

祖母说我可以在两个防波堤之间的海岸边来回走。这些防波堤是用岩石建成的，一直延伸到海里。祖母说建防波堤是为了避免海滩被侵蚀掉。

---

siren *n.* 警报声
jetty *n.* 防波堤

tickle *v.* 发痒

the ocean. Gram said the jetties were built to keep the beach from *eroding* away. She said that a long time ago the beaches were much larger, so the town built the jetties to keep the sand from flowing away into the ocean.

Gram said I could not go into the water unless she or Jim was with me. She told me about currents, the strong flow of water, and how they could pull me under and drag me far out into the ocean. She told me if I learned the rules, I would also learn to love the ocean. The ocean was one of Gram's best friends.

After a delicious dinner of crab cakes, I went upstairs to go to bed. The sounds were new. The shadows were new. The smells were new. The waves beating, beating, beating onto the shore *lulled*

她说在很久以前海滩比现在大很多，因此城镇建造了防波堤阻止沙子向大海里流失。

祖母说没有她或是吉姆的陪伴，我是不能到水里去的。他跟我讲述了关于洋流的知识，一种强大的水流，它们可以把我拉入水下，并远远地把我拖向大海深处。她告诉我如果学会了大海的法则，我也同样会学会热爱大海。大海是祖母最好的朋友之一。

在一顿美味可口的蟹饼晚餐之后，我上楼去睡觉。声音是新鲜的，影像是新鲜的，连味道都是新鲜的。海浪在岸上拍打着，拍打着，拍打着，

---

erode *v.* 腐蚀

lull *v.* 使镇静

me to sleep.

Limulus

I awoke with the sun shining onto my face. I could hear birds *screeching*—seagulls? I hurriedly pulled on shorts and a T-shirt. Gram said to remember the rules. I nodded yes, as I hurried out the back door.

The sand had many brownish-gray round things all over it. They kind of looked like turtles but not quite. They had a pointed tail sticking out of them that looked sharp. Others were lying on their shelled backs. I watched some of them for a while until Gram called me for breakfast.

I asked Gram what was all over the beach, and she said they

催我进入了梦乡。

鲎

洒在脸上的阳光让我醒来。我能听到鸟儿的鸣叫声——是海鸥吗？我匆匆穿上短裤和一件T恤。祖母说要记住大海的法则。我一边点头说是，一边急匆匆地跑出了后门。

沙滩上遍布着许多灰褐色圆圆的东西。它们看起来有点儿像乌龟，但又不完全像。尖尖的尾巴从它们的身体伸出，看起来非常尖锐。有一些甲壳朝下仰面躺在沙滩上。我观察了它们中的一些好一阵子，直到祖母喊我回去吃早饭。

我问祖母遍布在海滩上的东西是什么，她告诉我它们是节肢动物，

---

screech *v.* 尖叫

were arthropods called horseshoe crabs. As I ate my cereal, she told me more about them. She said scientists call them limuli, but because of their shape, most people call them horseshoe crabs. The waves take the horseshoes back into the water. I told Gram about the ones turned upside down in the sand. Gram said that they use their tail to try to turn themselves upright. If they weren't able to, they'd die and become food for other animals. Gram also said we did not eat limuli in our crab cakes last night.

I asked how horseshoe crabs survive. Gram told me that many are *stranded* on the beach after the tide *recedes*. They try to escape from the sun's heat by *burrowing* into the wet sand. She said the females do not lay eggs until they are 10 years old and they often live for 18 years. Gram said they lay their green jelly-looking eggs a

---

叫作马掌蟹（英语直译过来时"马掌蟹"，其实不是蟹类，而是形状像是马掌的鲎）。我一边吃着麦片粥，她一边告诉我关于它们更多的东西。他说科学家叫它们鲎，但是因为它们的外形，多数人叫它们马掌蟹。海浪会把这些"马掌"带回到水中。我告诉祖母关于那些在沙滩上"翻个儿"的"马掌"。祖母说它们试着用尾巴把自己翻过正面来。如果它们没有办法翻过来，它们会死去，成为其他动物们的美餐。祖母还说昨晚我们吃的蟹饼里可没有鲎。

我问那些马掌蟹要如何才能幸存下来。祖母告诉我在潮汐退去以后，海滩上会有许多马掌蟹搁浅。为了尽量躲避太阳的热量，它们会挖洞钻进潮湿的沙子里面。她说它们通常会活十八年，而雌性在十岁以前是不产卵

---

strand *v.* 使搁浅   recede *v.* 后退
burrow *v.* 挖洞

few inches under the wet sand, and a female might lay as many as 80,000 eggs in one season.

Gram said that within two weeks, the larvae that develop from the eggs that aren't eaten by birds wash out to the ocean. The *larvae* are tailless but after their first *molt*, toward the end of summer, the larvae develop a tail. The ones that were not eaten in the sea grow into male and female limuli. She said they continue to grow and molt several times during the year for the first three years. Then they molt each year until they are fully grown at about age 12.

"What is 'molt'?" I asked Gram.

"Molt means an animal sheds its skin, or fur, or feathers, and then grows back new ones. Often this happens because the animal is growing larger."

的。祖母告诉我它们在湿沙下面几英寸的地方产下看起来像果冻一样的绿色的卵，而一个季度雌蟹可以产下多达八万枚卵。

祖母还说，不到两周，那些没有被鸟儿吃掉的卵就会发育成幼虫，然后冲落到大海。幼虫是没有尾巴的，但到夏天快结束的时候，它们第一次脱皮以后，幼虫就长出了尾巴。在大海里没有被吃掉的那些会长成雄性和雌性的鲎。她告诉我它们会不断成长，在头三年每一年里都会脱几次皮。然后在十二岁完全成长之前，它们每年脱一次皮。

"什么是脱皮？"我问祖母。

"脱皮的意思是，动物脱掉它的外皮或毛皮或者羽毛，然后再长出新的来。因为动物在不断长大所以这种情况经常发生。"

---

larvae *n.* 幼虫　　　　　　　　　　　　　　　　　　molt *n.* 脱皮

Then we walked to the beach so I could learn more.

Gram said she always put the stranded female horseshoe crabs back into the ocean. She would also turn over the upside down ones because if their undersides became too dry they would die.

She said while they swim, horseshoe crabs often turn on their backs floating on their shell as if it were a boat. After swimming for a while, they stop to rest and gradually sink to the bottom of the ocean. As they move along the bottom, they eat a variety of soft-shell *clams*, *marine* worms, surf clams, small *invertebrates*, and *algae*. Since they grind food with their spiny leg segments, they have to be walking to chew their food.

Gram also said they prefer living as bottom dwellers because of

---

于是我们走向海滩，这样我能学到更多东西。

祖母说她经常把搁浅的雌马掌蟹放回大海。她还会把"翻个儿"的那些给翻过来，因为如果它们的底面太干的话它们会死的。

她还说当它们游泳的时候，马掌蟹经常会翻转过来，用它们的壳像一只船那样漂流。游了一段时间以后，它们会停下来休息并且渐渐地沉到海底。当它们在海底前行时，会吃各种各样的软壳蚌，海虫，蛤蜊，小的无脊椎动物，还有藻类。当它们用腿多刺的部分去磨碎食物时，不得不边前行边咀嚼食物。

祖母又说因为海水的高含盐度它们更喜欢作为海底生物。到了冬天，

---

clam *n.* 蚌
invertebrate *n.* 无脊椎动物

marine *adj.* 海洋的
alga *n.* 海藻

the high salt content. In the winter, they burrow down into the mud of the ocean floor.

Other animals try to destroy them, and scientists study them to learn more about their nine eyes and nerve systems. Also, limuli blood can be used to test for some human diseases and to test new drugs. Some farmers even *grind* them up to feed their hogs. Amazingly, Gram said horseshoe crabs have been around for 350 million years—since dinosaurs roamed the earth.

Rescuing

So every morning I hurried to the beach to save as many horseshoe crabs as I could. I would turn them over, if seagulls hadn't reached. Then I'd pick them up and toss them into the

---

它们会挖洞钻入海底的泥里。

其他的动物试图消灭它们，而科学家们则通过研究想更多了解它们的九只眼睛和神经系统。还有鲎的血液用来检测一些人类的疾病，还可以用来检测新药。一些农民甚至把它们磨碎了去喂猪。令人惊讶的是，祖母说马掌蟹已经存活了大约三亿五千万年——从恐龙遍布地球的时代就已经存在。

营救

于是早上我都会急匆匆地跑去海滩，去营救尽可能多的马掌蟹。如果海鸥没有先我到达开始吃它们脆弱的部分，我就会把它们翻过来，然后把

---

grind *v.* 磨碎

waves. Many times they'd float back in and become stuck on the shore again, but I soon learned when the waves would take them farther out into the water. Sometimes I'd take them to the end of the jetty, *toss* them into the waves and wish them "good luck" as the horseshoe crabs floated away. I also tried to chase birds away when I saw them reaching into the sand with their *beaks* to eat the eggs. Gram told me I should leave the birds alone because for many years this has been their way of getting food to eat on their flight back north.

One morning I ran to the beach and there was not a horseshoe

它们捡起来投进海浪里。很多时候他们会漂回来再次困在岸边，但我很快了解到何时海浪能把它们更远地带回水里。有时我要把它们带到防波堤的末端，投进海浪里，当马掌蟹漂走了，我会祝它们"好运"。当看到鸟儿用它们的喙伸到沙子里吃卵时，我还试着把鸟赶走。祖母告诉我不要去干涉鸟儿们，因为多年来这都是鸟儿们在飞回北方的迁徙途中的觅食方法。

　　一天早上，我跑到海滩，而那儿却连只马掌蟹都看不到了。我上气不接下气地跑回房子，问祖母它们都哪儿去了！她说它们的产卵期已经结束

---

toss　*v.* 投

beak　*n.* 鸟喙

crab in sight. I breathlessly ran back to the house and asked Gram where they were. She said that their time for laying eggs was finished. Next year many more limuli would come on shore to lay their eggs. I just hoped I would be there to save them.

I walked back to the beach. I lay down upon the warm damp sand, *shielding* my eyes from the bright morning sun. My summer vacation had just begun. What would I do now? Maybe I should tell Gram about the Ants in My Bed!

了。明年会有更多的鲎来到岸边产卵的。我真希望我会在那儿营救它们。

我走回海滩。躺在温暖潮湿的沙子上，手搭凉棚遮挡早晨明亮的阳光。我的暑假才刚刚开始。现在我要做什么呢？也许我应该跟祖母说说我床上的蚂蚁！

---

shield *v.* 遮住（眼睛）

6

Grandpa—Smoke Jumper

Chapter One

"**A**re we there yet?" my sister asked for the seventh time in less than thirty minutes.

"Not for another twenty minutes or so," Mom answered with more patience than I had left.

I was bored, *cranky*, and not exactly looking forward to a weekend

---

爷爷——空降消防员

第一章

"**我**们还没到吗？"在不到三十分钟的时间里，我的妹妹已经问了七遍这个问题了。

"再有差不多二十分钟就到了。"妈妈比我更有耐心地回答道。

我觉得很无聊，暴躁，而且根本就不期待在祖父母家度过周末。他们

---

cranky *adj.* 脾气坏的

at the grandparents' in Cave Junction, Oregon. What kind of a name for a town is that anyway? I thought as I *pursed* my lips and stared blankly out of the car window, thinking about the million other things I'd rather be doing at this particular moment.

"Whoa, what on earth is that?" I leaned forward in my seat, *startled* by the huge tower *looming* before us. My sister, Karen, *craned* her neck to see what I was pointing at, crossing our boundary and invading my space. I did not care, as I was too preoccupied with the massive structure that had suddenly appeared.

"I believe that's one of the old smoke-jumper towers, Andy," Mom answered.

的家在俄勒冈州的临洞。对于一个城镇来说这是个什么名字啊？我一边想一边紧闭着嘴唇呆呆地望着窗外发愣，考虑着在这个特殊时刻我宁愿去做的无数的其他事情。

"哇，那到底是什么啊？"我从座椅上将身体向前倾，被赫然出现在我们面前的巨大高塔所震惊。我的妹妹，凯伦，越过我们之间的界线，侵占着我的空间，伸长了脖子去看我所指的东西。因为我是如此全神贯注于突然出现的宏伟建筑，所以根本没有在意她的举动。

"我认为那是过去空降消防员的一个空中跳台，安迪。"妈妈回答说。

---

purse *v.* 噘嘴
loom *v.* 出现

startled *adj.* 吃惊的
crane *v.* 伸（颈）

"What's a smoke jumper?" I asked as I leaned out the window to look up at the thing towering above me like some ancient wooden giant. A couple of the *timbers* were *rotting*, and they looked as if they had been abandoned for years.

"Smoke jumpers are a group of highly trained people who jump out of airplanes to fight wildfires," Mom explained. "There used to be a smoke-jumping *base* here in Cave Junction."

I twisted in my seat to look back at the tower, which was quickly *diminishing* behind us as we drove away.

"You should ask Grandpa to tell you about it; he used to be a smoke jumper," Mom added when I settled back down.

She must be pulling my leg, I thought. I couldn't even picture Dad as a smoke jumper, much less Grandpa; the idea was just too

---

"什么是空降消防员？"我一边问一边将身体探出窗外，抬头仰望着，就像是古代的木头巨人一样高耸入云的家伙。几根木料已经腐烂，看起来已经被废弃多年了。

"空降消防员是一群训练有素的人，他们跳出飞机从天而降，去扑救森林大火。"妈妈解释道："在临洞这里曾经有过一个空降消防基地。"

我在座位上扭转身体向后看着高塔，当我们的车越驶越远，那高塔在我们身后也迅速地越变越小。

"你应该让爷爷告诉你有关它的事情，他曾经是一名空降消防员。"当我又重新回到座位上坐好后，妈妈补充道。

我想，她一定是在跟我开玩笑。我甚至不能想象爸爸要是一名空降消防员会是什么样子，更别说爷爷了，这想法实在是太可笑了。但是如果妈

---

timber *n.* 木材
base *n.* 基地

rot *v.* 腐烂
diminish *v.* 减小

ridiculous. But what if Mom was telling the truth? I wondered if Grandpa really was a smoke jumper.

"Are we there yet?" I asked, anxious to get some answers.

Chapter Two

As soon as Dad stopped the car, I jumped out and headed straight for the house. "Hey, hold on a minute, Andy, come back and help with the bags," Dad said, stopping me in my tracks.

I *groaned* in frustration. I knew I was supposed to help Dad with the bags, but I desperately wanted to find out what Grandpa knew about the smoke jumpers. As I stood there debating what to do, Grandma rushed out of the door.

妈讲的都是真的该怎么办？我真的很想知道爷爷过去是否真是一名空降消防员。

"我们还没到吗？"我问道，急切地想要得到一些答案。

第二章

爸爸刚停下车，我便从车里跳了出来，径直朝着爷爷奶奶的房子跑去。"嘿，稍等一下，安迪，回来帮助拿行李。"爸爸的话让我停下了脚步。

我沮丧地抱怨着。我知道我本应该帮助爸爸拿行李的，但是我真的是太想知道爷爷关于空降消防员都知道些什么了。就在我站在那儿争辩着做些什么的时候，奶奶从门里奔了出来。

---

groan *v.* 抱怨

"You're finally here!" she exclaimed joyfully from the front porch. Grandpa walked by her and *limped* down the stairs, tightly *gripping* the *rail* for balance.

There's no way he could have jumped out of airplanes and fought fires, I thought to myself. My excitement was gone. I turned around and went back to help Dad with the bags.

It was hotter inside the house than it was outside. The windows were all open, desperately encouraging the breezes to come in, but so far none had accepted the invitation. I paced back and forth restlessly. Mom and Grandma were busy chatting in the kitchen as they prepared dinner. Dad was in the living room discussing his latest project with Grandpa, and Karen was sitting on the porch

---

"你们终于到了！"她从前门廊那儿高兴地呼喊着。爷爷走在她身旁，蹒跚着走下楼梯，紧紧地抓住栏杆以保持平衡。

我心想，说什么他都不可能从飞机里跳出来和火灾搏斗的。我激动的心情全都消失了，我转过身来走回去帮着爸爸拿行李。

屋子里面比外面还要热。窗户全都打开了，拼命地鼓励着让微风吹进来，但迄今为止还没有一点微风接受了邀请。我躁动不安地来回踱着步。妈妈和奶奶在厨房里忙着聊天准备晚餐。爸爸在客厅和爷爷讨论着他的最新项目，而凯伦则坐在"像秋千"的廊椅上给她三个最喜爱的洋娃娃讲故事。

---

limp *v.* 跛行　　　　　　　　　　　　　　　　grip *v.* 紧握
rail *n.* 栏杆

swing reading a story to her three favorite dolls.

I was just bored out of my mind, wandering aimlessly through the house, stopping every now and then to inspect objects from the past that adorned my grandparents' home. In one room I found an old *push-pedal* sewing machine that Grandma apparently still used, since there was a pile of clothes in a basket next to it. In another room I discovered an old *turntable* with a *stack* of faded cardboard record jackets.

"Haven't they heard of CDs?" I muttered, absently *flipping* through the stack of unfamiliar musicians. I quickly got bored with them and opened the door to the library.

There was a multitude of photographs in the room. Some were

我无聊得简直受不了了，漫无目的地在屋子里闲逛，时不时地停下来观察一下用来装饰祖父母房子的老古董。在一间屋子里我发现了一个古老的脚踏缝纫机，奶奶很显然还在用它，因为在它旁边的篮子里还放了一堆衣服。在另外一间屋子里我发现了一张古老的唱机唱盘和一摞已经褪了色的硬纸板唱片套封。

"他们难道没有听过激光唱片吗？"我喃喃自语道，心不在焉地翻阅着这并不熟悉的音乐家的唱片。很快我就对这些唱片感到厌倦了，于是打开房门去了书房。

房间里有许多照片。有些是黑白的，另外那些则已经褪色变成了棕褐

---

push-pedal *n.* 推板
stack *n.* 一叠

turntable *n.* （唱机的）唱盘
flip *v.* 翻动

black and white, and others were brown and faded, and they *resided* on shelves, tables, and walls. I *skimmed* over the photographs, not really paying much attention to their content, since they were mostly of people I did not know. One photograph, however, made me stop in my *tracks*. It was a group shot of about twenty men in front of an airplane and a sign that read "Gobi Smoke Jumper Base."

"Oh my goodness, Mom wasn't kidding." Excited, I grabbed the photograph and ran out of the room.

Chapter Three

"Grandpa, were you a smoke jumper?" I burst into the living room

---

色，而且它们在书架上，桌子上，还有墙上摆得到处都是。我快速浏览着照片，并没有完全在意照片的内容。因为照片上大多都是我不认识的人。但是，有一张照片让我停了下来。这是一张大约有二十几个人在一架飞机前的集体照，还有一块牌子，上面写道："戈壁空降消防员基地。"

"哦，我的天呐，妈妈没有开玩笑。"我兴奋极了，抓起照片跑出了房间。

第三章

"爷爷，你曾是名空降消防员吗？"我闯进了客厅并把照片递给了

---

reside *v.* 存在于

skim *v.* 浏览

track *n.* 足迹

and handed him the photograph. He looked down at the picture and slowly began to trace the faces with his finger, and a smile played about his mouth as he looked back up at me.

"I sure was, Andy," he said as he pointed to one of the faces in the group. "That's me right there."

I leaned closer to examine the face. The young man smiling back at me looked a lot like my dad. I looked down at Grandpa, but I didn't see much of a *resemblance*.

"Of course, that was quite a few years ago," Grandpa added with a chuckle.

I took the photo from him and flopped down on the floor. I could not make the connection between the young man in the photo and the old man sitting in the chair before me.

他。他低头看着照片，并开始用手指慢慢地映描着照片上的一张张面孔，当他再抬起头来看着我的时候，嘴角挂满了微笑。

"当然了，安迪。"他边指着集体照里众多面孔中的一个边说。"就在那里，那就是我。"

我靠近一些仔细看那个面孔。照片上年轻人微笑着回敬我，看起来像极了我的爸爸。我低头看着爷爷，却看不出多少相似之处。

"当然了，那是好多年前的事了。"爷爷轻声笑着补充说道。

我从他那儿拿回照片，一屁股坐到地板上。我实在无法把照片中的年轻人和这位坐在我面前椅子上的老人联系起来。

---

resemblance *n.* 相似之处

"We saw a smoke-jumper tower on the drive over," Karen announced as she made herself comfortable in Dad's lap.

"We used to practice jumping off those towers before we went up in the airplanes," Grandpa explained.

That was all it took; I could no longer contain my curiosity. "You jumped off those things?" I burst out in amazement. "They're so HUGE! What was it like, Grandpa? You know, jumping out of planes, fighting fires?" The *barrage* of questions literally flew out of my mouth.

Grandpa smiled and settled back into his chair. He had a *captive* audience and a very good story to tell.

"在我们驱车来的路上看到了一个空降消防员的空中跳台。"当凯伦让自己舒舒服服地坐在爸爸的腿上之后述说着。

"过去在我们登上飞机之前，我们经常练习从那些高塔上跳下来。"爷爷解释道。

那就是它的一切了，我无法再克制我的好奇心。"你从那些东西上跳下来吗？"我吃惊地大声喊道。"它们是如此巨大！爷爷那是什么样的感觉？你知道的，就是从飞机里跳出来，和大火搏斗的感觉？"这些接二连三的问题简直是从我的口中飞出来一样。

爷爷微笑着又坐回到他的椅子上。他有了一个忠实的听众，而且他有一个很好的故事要讲。

---

barrage *n.* 接二连三的一大堆（质问或指责等）　　　　captive *adj.* 无权选择的

Chapter Four

"I was just eighteen years old when I became a smoke jumper," he began. "It was the summer of 1946, and the previous year my buddies Charlie, Greg, and I signed up for smoke-jumper training. Everyone thought we were crazy for wanting to jump out of planes and fight fires."

He shook his head and laughed at the memories that came back. "You had to be in top physical condition to be a smoke jumper," Grandpa continued. "The test was *grueling*. Hard to imagine now, but back then I could do twenty-five push-ups, forty-five sit-ups, and

第四章

"当我成为一名空降消防员的时候，我只有十八岁。"他开始讲述他的故事。"那是在1946年的夏天，在前一年我和我的好朋友查理还有格雷格一起报名参加了空降消防员的培训。跳出飞机与火灾搏斗的想法让大家都觉得我们疯了。"

他摇了摇头，嘲笑着那段被唤起的回忆。"要成为空降消防员你必须有一流的身体条件。"爷爷继续说道："那测试让人筋疲力尽。现在很难想象，但回想当年我能在不到九十分钟里做二十五个俯卧撑，四十五个仰

grueling *adj.* 使人筋疲力尽的

pack over a hundred pounds of *gear* three miles in less than ninety minutes."

He chuckled again. "Oh, it was a very tough course. Charlie dropped out after the first week and trained instead to be a *spotter*; turned out he made the right decision, since he was the best darn spotter in the *business*."

"Spotter?" I was about to ask what a spotter was when Grandpa started back in on the story.

"Charlie called it in at about 5 A.M. He'd spotted a fire from one of the towers and alerted Jack, the fire chief, and by 5:30 we were all at the base listening as Jack briefed us on the situation."

He paused for a second and Dad took the opportunity to explain.

卧起坐，并且背上超过一百镑的装备走上三英里。"

他轻声笑了笑继续说道："哦，那是个非常艰难的历程。查理在头一个星期以后退出了，转而训练成为一名火点观察员。结果表明他做出了正确的决定，后来他成为这一行里最好的火点观察员。"

"火点观察员？"我正要问火点观察员是什么的时候，爷爷又重新开始讲他的故事了。

"查理在大概早上五点时打来电话。他从其中的一个塔台观测到一处火点，并向消防队长杰克发出了警报，在五点半之前我们全部到达基地，听取杰克向我们做的关于火情的简报。"

他暂停了片刻，而爸爸正好利用这个机会向我解释道："作为火点观察

---

gear *n.* 装备

business *n.* 行业

spotter *n.* 侦查员

"The spotter looks for fires and decides where the smoke jumpers need to go and where they are going to land."

"I probably should explain first that it was late August, and we were *smack* in the middle of peak fire season," Grandpa continued. "It hadn't rained in over a month, the temperatures were averaging ninety degrees daily, and we were making jumps practically every week."

"However," he stated *emphatically*, "no one expected the fire we faced that day. By 6 A.M., Greg and I were crammed like *sardines* with the rest of the smoke jumpers in the belly of the DC-3 airplane. Charlie relayed information from the open doorway at the back to the pilots in the *cockpit*, and they responded immediately, banking

---

员要搜索火灾，并且要决定空降消防员需要去哪里和他们要在哪里着陆。"

"我或许应该首先说明一下，那是八月底，我们正置身于火险的最高峰季节。"爷爷继续说道："已经有一个多月没有下雨了，每天的平均气温达到九十华氏度，而我们几乎每个星期都要空降灭火。"

"然而，"他强调地陈述着："没有人料到那天我们所面临的那场森林大火。不到早上六点钟，格雷格还有我和其他空降消防员一起像沙丁鱼挤满在DC-3型飞机的肚子里（机舱里）。查里从机舱后部开着的舱门到驾驶舱给飞行员传递着信息。他们迅速做出了反应，向左倾斜转向，朝着选

---

smack *adv.* 恰好
sardine *n.* 沙丁鱼

emphatically *adv.* 强调地
cockpit *n.* （飞机的）驾驶舱

left to head to the selected drop target."

"'FIRST STICK, UP!' Charlie shouted, and our crew of four men headed over to the open doorway. I snapped in my static line, got a fix on the jump spot, and leapt out of the plane, *plummeting* to the ground at an alarming speed." Grandpa's voice rose with excitement.

"The wind *whipped* at my face and *tugged* at my mouth as I counted, 'One, one thousand, two, one thousand, three.' Then WHOOSH!" He flung his arms up over his head. "The parachute snapped open, abruptly halting my descent and, sending my legs flying up over my head. I *spun* around and around, spiraling

---

定的空降目标上空飞去。"

"'第一队，起立！'查理喊道，我们一组四名成员起身来到打开的舱门处。我咔嗒一声把弹簧、搭苟扣在了我的降落伞固定拉绳上，定位了空降着陆点，然后从飞机上一跃而下，以惊人的速度朝地面垂直下落。"由于激动，爷爷的嗓音越提越高。

"风就像是鞭子一样抽打着我的脸，在我数秒的时候，风使劲地拉扯着我的嘴巴。'一个，一千，两个，一千，三个。'接着嗖的一声！"他把胳膊猛地甩过头顶。"降落伞啪的一声打开了，骤然中止了我的急速下降，使我的腿一下子飞过了头顶。我一圈又一圈地旋转着螺旋式地下降，

---

plummet *v.* 速降
tug *v.* 使劲拉

whip *v.* 鞭打
spin *v.* 快速旋转

downward through, the smoke and heading right toward the flames. *Instinctively* I shifted my weight left and right until I regained control and *maneuvered* my *chute* toward the jump spot, where I hit the ground with a bone-crushing thud."

Grandpa paused for a moment, looking a bit worn out from the excitement of the jump. I hoped he wasn't going to stop now.

"One by one the others in my group landed around me, followed by our gear," he continued in a softer voice. "We quickly strapped the hundred pounds of gear on our backs and *donned* our make-shift helmets. Five minutes ago we were safe in the belly of the plane that circled overhead, and now we were heading straight into the fire."

穿过烟雾，直朝着火焰就飞了过去。本能地，我左右来回变换重心，直到我又恢复了控制，操控着我的降落伞飞向空降着陆点，在那儿我重重地砸在地面上，那震击足以压碎骨头。"

　　爷爷暂停了一会儿，看起来这次跳伞的兴奋让他有点筋疲力尽了。我可不希望他现在停下来。

　　"我们小组的成员一个接着一个在我旁边降落了，随后是我们的装备。"他的声音柔和了一些继续说道："我们迅速把上百磅重的装备用皮带捆绑好背在后背上，戴上我们的临时头盔。五分钟以前我们还安全地待在盘旋在空中的飞机机舱里，而现在我们却朝着大火直冲了进去。"

---

instinctively *adv.* 本能地

chute *n.* 降落伞

maneuver *v.* 操控

don *v.* 戴上

Chapter Five

"The small fire that had started just over an hour before had grown quite rapidly in size and strength. Urged on by *gusting* winds and fueled by acres of crisp, dried grass, it had raced forward, jumping ditches and small streams and evolving into the raging wall of flames before us. Our job was to contain the fire *perimeter*, *extinguishing* all spot fires and *flare-ups*, which are little fires that start from the big fire and add to it, before they swept out of control. We put out a total of sixteen spot fires in three hours, succeeding in containing the fire in one area, but we were unable to put it out.

第五章

　　"一个小时以前还是刚刚开始的小火灾，现在不论是从规模上还是火势上都异常迅速地增大了。在狂风的驱策下，在满地又干又脆的草的作用下，大火跃过沟渠和小溪全速向前推进，进化成一道挡在我们面前的熊熊燃烧的火墙。我们的工作是控制火线长度，熄灭所有的飞火以及骤然火，它们是起步于大火灾的一些小火灾，而且能增强森林大火灾。在它们失去控制席卷开来之前我们必须消灭它们。在三个小时里，我们总共扑灭了十六处飞火，成功地把大火控制在一个区域，但我们却无法扑灭它。"

gust *v.* 猛吹
extinguish *v.* 熄灭

perimeter *n.* 边缘
flare-up *n.* 突发

"The fire inched closer and closer to the row of trees at the base of the mountain. Fingers of flame licked at the bark, igniting the trees one by one like they were candles on a birthday cake."

I wiped the sweat from my brow, imagining the heat of the fire.

"You think it's hot in here, boy," Grandpa looked over at me. "But nothing can prepare you for the heat of a wildfire. You don't just see the fire; you hear it, taste it, and feel it," he continued. "A *deafening* roar filled the air; it was as if a *freight* train were bearing down on us. The heat wrapped around us like a heavy blanket that immediately got *soaked* with the sweat streaming down our backs and faces. We were completely surrounded by smoke; our eyes burned and we *scorched* our throats every time we took a breath. We were running

---

"大火缓缓前进离山麓的一排树木越来越近。火舌舔舐着树皮，好像它们是生日蛋糕上的蜡烛一样，一个接着一个地将树木点燃。"

我擦了擦额头的汗水，想象着火的高温。

"孩子，你认为这里很热。"爷爷朝我看过来。"但你怎么能无法想象森林大火的温度。你不仅仅是看到大火，还可以听到它，尝到它，甚至感受到它。"他继续说："空气中弥漫着震耳欲聋的轰鸣声，就好像是一辆货运列车在向我们迅速逼近。高温像一条厚厚的毯子一样紧紧地包围着我们，汗水像河水一样从后背和脸上流下，立刻就让我们湿透了。我们完全被烟雾所包围；我们的眼睛灼痛，每喘一口气都会灼伤我们的喉咙。

---

deafening *adj.* 震耳欲聋的
soaked *adj.* 湿透

freight *n.* 货运
scorch *v.* 烫坏；烤焦

out of air, the fire was sucking up all the oxygen, and the clouds of black smoke began *spiraling* upward in search of the fresh air we so desperately needed... not a good sign."

Grandpa leaned over and took the photograph from my hands. I was *gripping* it so hard that I'd almost *cracked* the glass. It was a good thing he took it away from me, because the story got even more intense.

'CROWN FIRE!' the line *scout* yelled, and I looked up in time to see flames bursting from the clouds of smoke just five feet above my head. Once the fire reaches the crowns of the trees, it leaps from tree to tree in midair, and almost nothing can stop it. The foreman

---

我们就要耗尽空气了，大火吸收了所有的氧气，而滚滚黑烟刚开始螺旋上升，以搜寻我们极度需求的新鲜空气了……这可不是什么好兆头。"

爷爷弯下身子，并从我手中拿过照片。我把它抓得太紧了，差点弄裂了相框玻璃。他把照片从我手中拿走是件好事，因为故事接下来变得更加紧张激烈了。

"树冠火！"火灾控制线侦察员大喊，我及时抬头望去，看到火焰从我头顶仅仅五英尺的滚滚浓烟里喷了出来。一旦大火到达了树木的树冠部分，它就会从半空中在棵棵树木之间跳跃，那几乎就没有什么可以阻止它的了。组长立即下令要我们全部向疏散通道出发。我们已经无能为力了，

---

spiral *v.* 盘旋上升（或下降）

crack *v.* 使破裂

grip *v.* 紧握

scout *n.* 侦察员

issued orders rapidly as we all headed for our escape routes. There was nothing we could do but hope that the *crews* ahead of us were successful in creating the backfire. It was the only way to stop a *crown* fire, and our only hope of saving the town of Goldberg."

"Did you save the town, Grandpa?" Karen asked anxiously.

"Shhh." I *scowled* at her for interrupting the story at such a critical point.

Thankfully, Grandpa continued. "The two fires, the wildfire and the backfire that had been set, approached each other like longtime enemies. They roared noisily, battling over who had the right of way. *Flames* rose into the air like arms as they each tried to push

---

只有希望我们前面的组员能成功地制造出"迎面火"。它是能够阻止树冠火的唯一途径了，也是我们挽救戈德堡镇的唯一希望了。

"你们挽救了城镇吗，爷爷?"凯伦急切地问道。

"嘘……"因为在最紧要关头打断了故事，我面带怒色地看着她。

幸好，爷爷仍在继续讲他的故事。"两股大火，那森林大火和已经被设置好了的迎面火，像是一对宿敌一样向彼此靠近。他们咆哮着，为了谁有权通行而争斗。它们都想使劲把自己向前推进，那火焰像胳膊一样耸立直冲空中。噼啪作响，火星四溅，它们继续战斗着，渐渐地丧失了力量并

---

crew *n.* 工作人员

scowl *v.* 对……沉下脸

crown *n.* 树冠

flame *n.* 火焰

their way forward. *Crackling* and *sparking*, they continued the fight, gradually losing strength and slowly wearing each other down. They had both left behind a trail of destruction, and since there was nothing left to feed the fires, they both eventually burned out."

"Yippee, you saved the town, Grandpa!" Karen clapped her hands.

"Yes, we did," Grandpa smiled. "The jump was a success. We had saved the town of Goldberg."

"Success?" I didn't share my sister's reaction. "What about the thousands of acres of land that were destroyed, Grandpa? Didn't anyone care about the land?" I demanded, completely *flabbergasted* that no one else seemed concerned about this matter.

且互相慢慢地消磨着。它们身后都留下了一条毁灭之路，由于没剩下任何可以供大火燃烧的东西了，它们最终都熄灭了。

"耶！你们挽救了城镇，爷爷！"凯伦高兴得直拍手。

"是啊，我们做到了。"爷微笑着说："那是次成功的空降。我们挽救了戈德堡镇。"

"成功？"我并没有去分享妹妹的反应。"爷爷，那些被毁掉的上千英亩的土地要怎么办？有人在意过那些土地吗？"我询问着，似乎没有其他人关心过这件事使我大吃一惊。

---

crackle *v.* 发出爆裂声   spark *v.* 点燃
flabbergasted *adj.* 大吃一惊；目瞪口呆

"Of course we cared, Andy. It would be close to impossible to find a smoke jumper who didn't care first and foremost about the land," Grandpa responded seriously. "But these were acts of Mother Nature, and Mother Nature always finds a way of taking care of herself. In fact, they're finding out that having a fire every once in a while is good for the land. Fires happen naturally, and when people keep preventing them and putting them out, more and more dead, dry material builds up. Then when a fire finally does come through, it's a *tragedy*."

"Believe me," he added, "I've seen my fair share of wildfires and witnessed firsthand the *resilience* of nature. I promise, fresh vegetation and new life does rise up from the ashes."

"我们当然在乎了，安迪。想找到一个不在乎土地的空降消防员几乎是不可能的。"爷爷严肃地回答道："但这些是大自然母亲的行为，而大自然母亲总会找到照顾她自己的办法。事实上，他们发现偶尔发生一次火灾对土地是有益的。火灾顺其自然地发生，而当人们一直防止火灾发生，并把它们扑灭，越来越多的死亡的和干燥的物质不断堆积。当一场火灾最终真的发生了，那可已经造成灾难了。"

"相信我。"他补充说："我想我看到的森林大火已经足够多的了，并且也亲身见证了自然的恢复能力。我保证，新鲜的植被和新的生命一定会从灰烬中重生的。"

---

tragedy *n.* 悲剧   resilience *n.* 快速恢复的能力

I was a little embarrassed by my *outburst*, but more amazed at how strongly I felt about protecting nature and its wildlife.

"Looks like there may be a bit of smoke jumper in you, Andy," Grandpa said proudly.

"Dinner's ready!" Grandma anncunced from the kitchen.

"Just in time," Grandpa said, rising *stiffly* from the chair and *rubbing* his belly.

Karen sprang from Dad's lap and raced down the hall, her bare feet *slapping* on the wood floors. The kitchen door slammed against the wall as she burst in. "Karen, don't run in the house," I heard Mom scolding. Dad and Grandpa shook their heads and laughed at

---

　　我的情感爆发让我觉得很难为情，但更多的是惊讶于我对保护自然和野生动物那种强烈的感觉。

　　"在你身上也许能看到一点空降消防员的影子，安迪。"爷爷自豪地说。

　　"晚餐准备好了！"奶奶在厨房里说道。

　　"正是时候。"爷爷说。他从椅子上僵硬地站起来，抚摸着他的肚子。

　　凯伦从爸爸的腿上一跃而起，跑向大厅，她光着脚丫拍打着木制的地板。当她闯进厨房，砰的一下把厨房的门摔到了墙上。"凯伦，不要在房子里面跑。"我听见妈妈训斥着。爸爸和爷爷摇了摇头，为我妹妹一直显示出来的活力而发笑。我从地板上拾起照片，跟着他们进到厨房。现在我

---

outburst　*n.*　（感情的）爆发　　　　　　　　stiffly　*adv.*　僵硬地
rub　*v.*　摩擦　　　　　　　　　　　　　　　slap　*v.*　啪的一声放下

the energy my sister always displayed. I picked up the photo from the floor and followed them into the kitchen. I could now see the resemblance between the young man in the photo and my Grandpa. I scanned the other faces, wondering which ones were Charlie, Jack, and Greg.

"Hey, Grandpa, who's the girl in this picture?" I asked as I *slid* into my seat.

"That's your grandma. Did I forget to mention that she flew the plane we jumped out of?" I stared *open-mouthed* at the tiny, gray-haired woman at the end of the table.

"Let's save that story for after dinner, Andy," Grandma suggested with a smile.

I smiled back. This weekend wasn't turning out to be so boring after all.

能看出照片里的年轻人和我爷爷的相似之处了。我浏览着其他的面孔，想知道哪一个是查理，杰克和格雷格。

"嘿，爷爷，这相片里的姑娘是谁？"当我的屁股刚刚落到椅子上，我便问道。

"那是你的奶奶啊。难道我忘记说了？我们就是从她驾驶的飞机里跳出来的。"我张大了嘴巴盯着在桌子末端那个小小的、头发花白的女人。

"让我们把那个故事留到晚餐后吧，安迪。"奶奶面带笑容地建议道。

我也笑着回应。这个周末毕竟没有如此无聊。

---

slide *v.* 滑动   open-mouthed *adj.* 张大嘴的；瞠目结舌的

7

Fishing in Simplicity

I live in Louisiana, not far from Lake Charles. It's a backwater kind of place surrounded by bayou and meandering molasses streams, water barely moving at all. The streams know they're eventually going to end up lost in the ocean—a drop in the *bucket*, so to speak—and they're in no hurry to get there. This is as good a place as any to *meander*, "this" being my hometown— Simplicity, Louisiana. There isn't much to the town. I guess that's why the name fits so well.

垂钓在简朴之城

我住在路易斯安那州,离莱克查尔斯不远的地方。那里有点闭塞,被牛轭湖(美国南部、尤指路易斯安那州的)和蜿蜒曲折、缓缓流淌的溪流所围绕,这里的水几乎不流动。溪流知道他们将抵达终点最终汇入大海——可谓是沧海一粟——而他们一点儿也不急于到达那里。这儿是个溪流蜿蜒的好地方,"这儿"就是我们的家乡——路易斯安那州,简朴之城。关于城镇没有太多可说的。我猜这就是为什么它的名字如此贴切了。

---

bucket *n.* 桶　　　　　　　　　　meander *v.* (河流、道路)蜿蜒而行

It was on these Simplicity backwaters when I was eight years old that I made what I thought was the most historical of discoveries. Any one of a hundred lazy summer nights, my granddaddy would tell the story of an old house lost in the *swamps* where slaves used to hide out before the Civil War. The old house is gone, but his story has it that the place kind of lights up once in a while, all filled with ghosts and such. The only *remnant* of the house is a staircase that seems to go nowhere. That's why, I suppose, they call it Nowhere House.

That's why, when I found an old stone staircase that *butted* up against a *sinkhole* filled with water that fed Syrup Creek, I thought for sure I had found Nowhere House. My granddaddy just laughed and

---

正是在这片闭塞的土地上，当我八岁的时候，我做出了我认为是简朴之城最具有历史意义的发现。在上百的任意一个懒洋洋的夏日夜晚，我的祖父都会讲一个关于一幢老房子消失在沼泽中的故事，这幢老房子在南北战争以前曾经是奴隶们的藏身之所。老房子已经不复存在了，但祖父的故事讲到它，说那个地方会时不时地有些光亮，满是幽灵和诸如此类的东西。唯一的房子残余是个看起来哪都去不了的楼梯。我认为那就是为什么他们叫它"不存在的房子。"

那就是为什么当我发现了一个古老的石头楼梯时，那楼梯高高翘起紧挨着一个由"糖浆小溪"的水注满了的蓄水池，我想我一定是发现了"不

---

swamp *n.* 沼泽

butt *v.* 突出

remnant *n.* 残余部分

sinkhole *n.* 落水洞；污水池

laughed. He said it was the old Deucane place that washed away in the flood of 63 years. There's nothing left except for thirteen steps up and a long drop to the water.

Fewer than a thousand people live in Simplicity, and most of them work for DeWilde's Feed and Seed or they don't work at all. Dewilde's does about everything: it's a flour mill where grain is ground, and they even have a shed out back where *cayenne* pepper is made into a hot sauce that would leave *blisters* on the sun. In front of the flour mill and *lumberyard* is the big store where you can buy anything and everything: a quart of fresh milk, barbecue sausages, *persimmons*, live crawdads, and even fishing tackle and lures.

It was the fishing tackle that drew me to DeWilde's. When I was

---

存在的房子"。我的祖父只是不停地笑啊笑。他说那就是老林肯的住所，在63年的洪水中被冲走了。除了十三级向上的台阶和一个到水面的长长的陡壁以外，什么都没剩下。

　　不到一千人生活在简朴之城，而大多数人都为德怀尔德饲料与种子公司工作，或者根本就不工作。德怀尔德几乎生产所有东西：它是一个面粉工厂，在那里谷物被磨碎加工。在面粉厂后面他们甚至还有一个把辣椒粉加工成辣酱的厂房，那辣酱辣得可以在太阳下留下烫伤的水疱。在面粉工厂和贮木场前面，有一个大商店，在那里你可以买到所有的东西：一夸脱鲜牛奶、烤肠、柿子、活的小龙虾，甚至钓鱼用具和鱼饵。

　　正是渔具和鱼饵吸引我去德怀尔德的。在我九岁的时候，我连一个子

---

cayenne *n.* 红辣椒　　　　　　　　blister *n.* （皮肤上摩擦或烫起的）水疱
lumberyard *n.* 贮木场　　　　　　　persimmon *n.* 柿子

nine, I didn't have two nickels to rub together, but that never stopped me from wishing up and down the fishing aisles.

Early spring of my tenth birthday, DeWilde's decorated the main window on the big front-porch side of the store with a fishing pole and all the rigging. It wasn't one of those long *cane* poles like my granddaddy used—it was a spinning reel with a pole made of *fiberglass*.

I wanted that pole in the worst of ways. Early in the morning before the sun heated everything beyond *intolerable*, I stood beside that window and stared. I don't know how many times I found myself standing there staring when I heard the school bell ring on the other side of town. I was late so many times that the *principal*, Mr. Dusard,

---

儿都没有，但那并不会阻止我往返在钓鱼之路上。

那是我十岁时的早春，德怀尔德给商店一侧大前廊的主窗口进行了装饰，用的是一支渔竿和所有的钓鱼装备。它可不是我祖父用的那种木制长钓竿——它是用玻璃纤维做成的渔竿，还带着卷线轮呢！

我非常想要那个渔竿。一大早上，炎热的太阳烤得一切都无法忍受，我就站在那橱窗旁边盯着看。不知道有多少次，当听到在小镇的另一端学校的铃声已经响起，我发现自己仍然站在那里盯着看。我迟到太多次了，以至于后来我们的校长杜萨德先生打了一张纸条，把我的名字贴在他办公

---

cane *n.* 竹竿

intolerable *adj.* 无法忍受的

fiberglass *n.* 纤维玻璃

principal *n.* 校长

taped a piece of paper with my name on it to the chair outside his office.

Now, I loved to fish—there was nothing better—but I didn't have a fancy *rig*. I only had a length of fishing line with a *bobber* and a barbless hook tied to the end. I always kept the line rolled up in my pocket because I just never knew when a fishing opportunity was going to happen.

Sometimes opportunity does knock, and when it does, you'd better open the door fast before it runs away. On Wednesday, two weeks after Easter, there was a sign at DeWilde's. The sign told of a catfish-catching contest. Not a big deal in Simplicity—we have catfish-catching contests all the time. What made this special was

---

室外的椅子上。

　　既然我很热爱钓鱼——没有什么比这更好的了——但我没有精致的装备。我所有的只是一段带浮标的渔线，还有个没有倒刺的渔钩绑在渔线末端。我总是会把这段渔线卷起来放进我的口袋里，因为我可不知道什么时候就会有个钓鱼的机会。

　　有的时候，机会确实会来敲门的，当它来了，你最好赶快把门打开，别让机会就这样溜走了。复活节两周后的星期三，德怀尔德打出了广告。广告上说会有一个钓鲶鱼大赛。在简朴之城这是个微不足道的事——我们时常会有钓鲶鱼比赛。但这次比赛特殊之处是它的奖品：正是那橱窗里的

---

rig *n.* 有专门用途的设备　　　　　　　　　bobber *n.* （钓鱼用的）浮子

the prize: the pole and reel in the window.

I may have only been ten years old, but I had a better feeling for catfish than any of the adults in town. Even my granddaddy said so, and that was hard for him because he was pretty good in his own right. He was *enchanted* by the competition himself. You see, he fished with a big old cane pole and a single line, and that fancy rig would do him real proud. It was my granddaddy who first taught me how to fish, but I kept on learning. That pole was going to be mine, and I told him so. So there ended up being a contest within the contest—me against my granddaddy. But my granddaddy never knew that I had a secret plan.

There were two basic rules: You could only catch one catfish

渔竿和渔具。

虽然我只有十岁，但要比起钓鲶鱼的感觉，我比镇上任何成年人都要好。甚至我的祖父也这样说。由于他自己钓鱼的本领也非常好，因此承认我钓鲶鱼好对他来说很不好接受。他本人对比赛也非常着迷。你要知道，他用来钓鱼的是又大又旧的木制钓竿，而且只有一条单一的渔线，而那精致的装备会让他无比自豪的。是我的祖父首先教我如何钓鱼的，而我一直在学习。那个渔竿将会属于我的，我也是这么告诉我的祖父的。所以钓鲶鱼大赛会以我和祖父之间的竞争而告终。但我的祖父不会知道我有一个秘密计划。

比赛有两条基本规则：在比赛当天你只能钓一条鲶鱼，而且是有时间

---

enchant *v.* 使入迷

fresh on the day of the contest, and there was a time limit. Since most folks who live here don't have a watch, the contest was ruled to be over half past dark, thirty minutes after sunset, no exceptions. In other words, if you were fishing and it got dark and all, you'd better *hightail* it to DeWilde's with whatever you had caught.

I got off to a really bad start. My granddaddy intentionally let me sleep in. He didn't try to wake me at all. He *brewed* himself a *thermos* of coffee and sneaked on down to the creek. I woke up sweating with the sun full on my face, a bad sign that it was ten o'clock or so. I should have given up on my secret plan then and there, but like my granddaddy, I'm not one to give up on much of anything. I pulled on some faded jeans, *yanked* on a T-shirt, and

---

限制的。因为大多数住在这里的人都没有手表，所以比赛规定在天黑后半个小时结束，也就是太阳落山以后三十分钟，无一例外。换句话说，如果你在钓鱼而天已经黑了，不管你钓到什么，你最好迅速跑回德怀尔德。

　　我真的有了一个很糟糕的开始。我的祖父故意让我睡过了头。他根本就没有试着叫醒我。他为自己冲好一保温瓶咖啡，偷偷地溜到小溪去了。当太阳照在脸上弄得我满头大汗的时候，我才醒过来，差不多十点钟了，真是个坏兆头。当场我应该放弃我的秘密计划了，但就像祖父一样，我对太多事情都不会放弃。穿上一件褪了色的牛仔裤，一把套上T恤衫，再把

---

hightail *v.* 迅速离开

thermos *n.* 热水瓶

brew *v.* 煮（咖啡）

yank *v.* 猛拉

rolled line into my pocket. I didn't wear shoes. It was hot, and I always thought shoes were bad luck anyway. I needed all the luck I could get now.

The slam of the screen door woke the neighbor's dog as I bolted from the house and *trotted* down Chigger Creek Lane. It wasn't much of a road, more of a dirt *rut* that wound through the swamp *cedar* and weeping *magnolia*. Along the way, I could hear granddaddy down at the creek laughing at me as I passed on by.

Though it was late, I stuck to my plan: fishing from the top step of the flooded Deucane place. I just had a feeling that there was a big cat there with my name on it, just like on my chair at the principal's office.

那卷起来的渔线塞进我的口袋。我都没有穿鞋。天气很热，而且我也一直认为鞋子会带来坏运气。现在我需要所有能得到的运气啊！

当我冲出房子，猛关上纱门，砰的声响把邻居家的狗都吵醒了，延着沙虱河小道我一路小跑。与其说那是条路还不如说那是穿过沼泽雪松和滴水栏的一条泥泞车辙。当我沿途路过祖父钓鱼的地方，听到他在下面的小溪边正嘲笑我呢！

尽管已经晚了，但我仍然坚持我的计划：在被冲走的林肯住所那儿，最上面的台阶垂钓。我有一种感觉，那儿有条大鲶鱼，而我的名字就在它身上，就像在校长办公室的椅子上有我的名字一样。

---

trot *v.* 小跑   rut *n.* 车辙

cedar *n.* 雪松   magnolia *n.* 木兰花

I climbed up the moss-covered stairs and pulled the line from my pocket. I sat down at the top, my legs *dangling* over, reflecting in the still waters of the sinkhole. I reached over and pulled back a slab of thick French moss. There, all white and juicy, were the biggest, *plumpest* grubs you ever saw. I *skewered* one onto my barbless hook and let it drop squiggling into the water. It sank from sight; the red and white bobber was the only sign that something was up.

I kind of *hunched* my shoulders and waited because that is the best thing and the only thing you can do if you're going to catch contest-winning catfish.

The sun bore down, crisping my face, and in the distance I could hear my granddaddy bragging about how he'd already won and that

---

　　我爬上了长满苔藓的楼梯，把那卷渔线从口袋里拽了出来。在楼梯顶我坐了下来，把腿悬在外面晃来晃去，景象倒映在蓄水池平静的水面上。我伸手够到一块厚厚的法国苔藓，向后拉把它掀开。那是你所见过最大最肥硕的蛆虫，白嫩多汁。我在没有倒刺的渔钓上穿一只，让它蠕动着落到水里。它从视野中消失沉入水里，现在露在水面上的唯一标示就是那红白相间的鱼漂了。

　　我稍稍耸了耸肩膀并开始等待，因为如果你想钓到赢得比赛的鲶鱼，那是你能做的最好的也是唯一的事情了。

　　太阳缓缓下沉，阳光把我的脸都烤脆了，在远处，我能听到祖父的声

---

dangle *v.* 悬挂；悬摆　　　　　　　　　　plump *adj.* 丰满的
skewer *v.* 用扦子串起　　　　　　　　　　hunch *v.* 耸起（双肩）

I might as well give up.

I never gave up. With the light slipping under the *bracken* and skipping off the black water, I changed *bait* for the eighth time without a nibble. Just as the sun dropped lower than my hopes, the bobber slowly slipped down in the water and disappeared deep. It was the hit I had been waiting for.

I let the line slip through my hands, patiently waiting to set the hook. When there was less than two feet of line left, I wrapped it around my right hand and *hauled* back hard. There was a return tug that nearly pulled me off the step, and then inch by inch I started reeling in that whale of a catfish. Old Moby was strong, and the skin on my hands was *shredded* like birthday ribbon where he pulled the

---

音，吹嘘着自己已经赢了，还有我可能还不如放弃什么的。

我决不放弃。随着鱼儿在欧洲蕨下面轻轻地滑动而后又偷偷地溜回深水去了，我只得第八次更换鱼饵，连一次小小的咬钓都没有。正当太阳落到比我的希望还低的时候，鱼漂慢慢地滑到水里而后深深地消失了。这正是我一直在等待的一次咬钓。

我让渔线在手中滑动，耐心地等待着渔钓钓牢。到还剩下不到两英尺的渔线时，我开始把线往右手上缠，并用力地往回拉。一个反方向的回拉力几乎把我拖下了台阶，然后我开始一点一点地把这条极大的鲶鱼钓了起来。老莫比非常强壮，我手上的皮肤，就是他拽着渔线从我手掌中拉过的

---

bracken *n.* 欧洲蕨   bait *n.* 鱼饵

haul *v.* （用力地）拉；拖   shred *v.* 切碎；撕碎

line through my palms.

By the time I got that *beast* out of the water, it was dark and I could barely see it, but my arms and back could feel the mighty weight. It was the fishing pole for sure. It being dark and all, I had less than thirty minutes to get to DeWilde's.

With the prize heavy on my back, I ran. I slipped three times, fell twice, and finally ripped up the steps of the Feed and Seed. Inside was packed with town folk. I must have been a sight to see—hands bleeding, jeans torn from falling—but I was there. From the looks of things, my catfish, Old Moby, was the biggest fish caught.

Later, there was no question that I had truly caught the biggest fish.

地方，被割得一条条的像生日彩带一样。

等到我把那怪兽拉出来水面的时候，天已经黑了，我几乎都看不到它了，但我的手臂和后背能感觉到那巨大的重量。它一定会为我赢得那渔竿的。天开始全黑了，我只有不到三十分钟的时间返回德怀尔德。

我背着能获得大奖的重量开始奔跑。我滑倒了三次，跌倒了两次，最后终于冲到了饲料与种子公司的台阶上。里面挤满了小镇上的人。我一定是看起来很可笑的人——手在流血，牛仔裤也摔破了——但我还是到了那里。从外观上看，我的鲶鱼，老莫比，是钓的鱼里最大的。

稍后，毫无疑问的，我确实钓到了最大的鱼。

---

beast *n.* 野兽

Later, there was no question that I truly was ten minutes late.

There was no question that my granddaddy won first prize with his *puny* little catfish that was half the size of Old Moby.

All in all, it still didn't end too badly. While the womenfolk cooked the catfish, men—grown men—gathered around me and *bragged* on my skill.

Kind of made me feel all grown up.

My granddaddy never found out that my secret plan was to give the pole to him anyway.

Things kind of always *work out* that way in Simplicity, my hometown.

同样，毫无疑问的，我确实迟到了十分钟。

还是毫无疑问的，我的祖父用一条还不到老莫比一半大的小鲇鱼赢得了第一名。

总而言之，这样的结局还不算太坏。当女人们开始煮鲇鱼时，男人们——成年的男人们——聚在我的周围并夸赞起我的钓鱼技术来。

这让我有点感觉彻底长大了。

我的祖父永远都不会发现我的秘密计划，事实就是不管怎么样都会把渔竿给他的。

事情总是会以差不多的方式得到解决，在简朴之城，我的家乡。

---

puny *adj.* 微小的　　　　　　　　　　　　brag *v.* 夸耀
work out 想出；得到（解决办法）

Miltie Math-head: Football Hero?

Being on the Team

At first look, you wouldn't think Milton Meyers, also known as Miltie Math-head, would turn out to be one of the best *quarterbacks* in the history of Cobb County Pee Wee Football. At age 12, he stood just 4 feet, 5.5 inches, which he, of course, rounded to 4 feet, 6 inches. After eating lunch, he weighed 70 pounds—fully dressed, in hiking boots, with a roll of quarters in his pocket.

It's true that some not-so-big kids are fast runners, such as

---

米泰——数学天才：橄榄球英雄？

加入球队

一看，你怎么也不会想到米尔顿·梅尔斯，即"数学天才米泰"，有一天会成为卡伯县比维橄榄球队史上最佳四分卫之一。年仅12岁的他只有4英尺5.5英寸的身高，四舍五入后也才4英尺6英寸。他吃过饭，全身球衣，穿上橄榄球鞋，口袋里再装一卷硬币——这样体重才70磅而已。

有些小块头的孩子的确要跑得快些，比如说吉米·戈登，而米泰就不

---

quarterback *n.* （美式橄榄球的）四分卫

Jimmy Gordon, but not Miltie. He was slower than *ketchup dribbling* out of a new bottle. At *tryouts*, Coach Jersinski clocked Miltie running the 40-yard dash in 7.4 seconds. Jimmy, of course, had the best time: 5.2 seconds. He also had one of his usual wise-guy lines.

"Hey, Miltie," he called out, "This is the 40- yard dash, not the 40-yard *dawdle*."

"Maybe Turtle Boy thought it was a nature walk," said Billy Beffalini, who we called "Beefalo" because everything about him was big and strong, even his breath.

The teasing had the guys rolling on the ground with laughter. I

行了。他的速度比刚开瓶的番茄酱滴出来的速度还要慢。预赛中，教练杰辛基让米泰短跑40码，他用了7.4秒。而吉米毫无疑问仍然用时最少：5.2秒。他还得加上一段挂在嘴边自诩聪明的台词。

"嘿，米泰，"他叫道，"这是40码的快速短跑，不是让你晃晃荡荡40码嘞。"

"也许海龟小子以为让他自在地散步呢。"比利·贝法里尼说道，我们叫他"皮弗娄牛"，因为任何和他有关的事情都很大很有力，连呼吸都不例外。

这一阵逗乐笑得大家在地上打滚。我觉得大家拿米泰寻开心不太合

---

ketchup *n.* 番茄沙司

tryout *n.* 选拔赛

dribble *v.* 使滴下

dawdle *n.* 游荡

knew it wasn't right to make fun of Miltie. He tried his best. Besides, he only came to tryouts because I asked.

The guys call me Dan-the-Man Dugan. I was the starting quarterback last year, but I've been Miltie's best friend a lot longer. We became *pals* in second grade when we both brought ant farms to school on Share Day—the same day Ms. Rayshap's class had a picnic.

You don't have to be a math-head to do the math here. Picnic plus ants equals disaster.

Miltie and I tease sometimes by calling each other "Ant Boy." Mary Beth Brady, who brought the *brownies* our ants crawled into,

---

适。他已经尽力了。而且，他是应我的要求才来参加预赛的。

　　大伙都叫我大男人丹·杜根。去年，我是四分卫的先发投手，但更早以前，我和米泰就是最好的朋友了。二年级的时候，我们在"分享日"那天都带了蚂蚁工坊去学校，那时我们就成了朋友。同一天，瑞夏普老师班上还去野餐了。

　　说到这里，不是天才也知道会发生什么了。野餐+蚂蚁=灾难。

　　我和米泰有时会互称"蚂蚁男"来逗乐。玛丽·贝斯·布雷迪，她带来的巧克力糕饼爬满了我们带的蚂蚁，我们每次拿这件事开玩笑她都恨得咬牙切齿，但我们也自从那时成了朋友。

---

pal *n.* 朋友　　　　　　　　　　　　　　brownie *n.* 巧克力蛋糕

hates it when we tease, but she's been our friend ever since.

"I don't know about being on the team, Danny," Miltie said. "When it comes to sports, I've got two left feet, two left hands, and ten left *thumbs*. The rest of your friends think I'm a loser."

"That can't be," I said, "because I'm a winner, and I wouldn't hang out with anyone who wasn't also a winner."

"That's because you know the real me, and they don't."

That's exactly why I wanted Miltie to be on the team. So everyone else—and maybe even Miltie— could see the Miltie I saw.

"Give them a chance to know the real you, Miltie," I said.

The new season started fine with four wins and one loss. Then

---

"丹尼，我不知道该不该加入球队，"米泰说，"一谈到运动，我的手脚就不听使唤了——就好像有两只左脚，两只左手，十个手指都变成了左手的大拇指。你的朋友们都认为我是个输家。"

"不会的，"我说，"因为我是赢家，和我在一起的人也肯定是赢家。"

"那是因为你了解我，但他们不了解。"

这就是我想让米泰加入球队的原因。这样所有的人都能看到我所认识的米泰，甚至米泰也可以重新认识自己。

"给他们一个了解你的机会吧，"我说。

新赛季开局还不错，四胜一负。但是队里的J教练总是谎话满天，一

---

thumb *n.* 大拇指

Coach J. hurt his back in a fishing accident, or playing golf. He kept changing the story. Either way, we needed a new coach. The only one who would step in at midseason was Old Man McGruder, who played football back in the days of leather helmets.

Mr. McGruder meant well. He gave us *pep* talks about teamwork and fighting spirit. He taught us neat, old-fashioned football plays like the "Statue of Liberty." But mostly, Mr. McGruder napped during our games.

Without a coach who was awake to call the plays, we ended up losing two games in a row. The rest of the season did not look good—until Miltie stepped in.

会说钓鱼时伤了后背，一会又说打高尔夫球时受了伤。不管他在哪儿受的伤，我们都得找个新教练。在赛季中，我们唯一能请到的也就只有迈克格鲁德老人了。他早在时兴皮革头盔的时候就开始玩橄榄球了。

迈克格鲁德的初衷是好的。他给我们讲团队合作和作战精神来给我们打气。他教我们巧妙的、老式的交锋策略，比如"自由女神像"姿势的传球。但大多数时候，他都会在我们比赛的时候打瞌睡。

比赛过程中缺少了教练的分析指导，我们连续两场比赛都以失败告终。本赛季余下的比赛情况也不太乐观——直到有了米泰的加入。

---

pep *n.* 活力；精力

Now, of course, it all makes sense. But at first, most of the players would have said the odds of Miltie leading our team to victory were one in a million. On the plus side, he was already our official team benchwarmer and water boy.

Miltie's Math Pays Off

Miltie's feet may not have been quick, but his brain sure was, especially with math. He could multiply four-digit numbers in his head faster than a *calculator*.

Jimmy, who almost failed math, *snorted* when I bragged about Miltie's math smarts. So, he challenged Miltie one day during *recess*.

现在当然可以说，米泰的加入意义重大。但最开始的时候，大多数球员都说米泰能带领我们队赢得比赛的概率微乎其微。不管怎么说，他已经是我们队正式的后备队员兼送水工了。

数学制胜

尽管米泰的腿脚不快，脑子却很灵活，特别是在数学方面。他能在脑子里快速地计算出四位相乘的数字，速度竟然比计算机还要快。

而数学几乎不及格的吉米在听到我吹嘘米泰的数学时显得很不屑。于是有一天在休息时，他向米泰发起挑战。

---

calculator *n.* 计算机
recess *n.* 休息期间

snort *v.* 轻蔑地哼

"Okay, Math-head, let's see how fast you really are." Jimmy pulled out a calculator. Beefalo called out the numbers.

"What's 1,234 times 5,678?"

"7,006,652," said Miltie.

"Unfair!" said Jimmy. "My finger slipped."

"Better not *blink* when Miltie is doing a math problem," I said.

"Ah, go back to that school for smart kids and let us regular kids play football," said Jimmy.

Miltie went to a math class at the community college one afternoon a week. It wasn't his fault he was great at math, but some of the guys wouldn't give him a break. We walked over to the

---

"好吧，数学天才，让我们见识见识你到底有多快。"吉米掏出一个计算器，由皮弗娄牛说数字。

"1234乘以5678等于多少？"

"7,006,652。"米泰答道。

"不公平！"吉米愤愤地说，"我的手指打滑了。"

"你最好在米泰做数学题的时候不要眨眼，"我建议道。

"噢，天才还是回学校吧，让我们这些普通的孩子在这里玩橄榄球，"吉米说。

米泰每周都有一个下午会去社区大学听数学课。擅长数学并不是他的错，但就是有人揪着这件事不放。为了躲开其他人，我们向滑板坡道走

---

blink *v.* 眨眼

skateboard *ramp* to get away from the others.

"They're just jealous," said Mary Beth. She saw the whole thing from the top of the skateboard ramp. "You know, you might win a few games if those guys knew as much about math as Miltie."

"Math?" I said.

"Math," said Mary Beth.

"Math!" *exclaimed* Miltie.

"Math?" I said, again.

"Miltie can use his math genius to design new plays," explained Mary Beth. "Football is all about math: angles, *arcs*, distance—"

"And the relationship between two points on a *grid*," added Miltie.

去。

　　"他们只是嫉妒罢了，"玛丽·贝斯说。她在滑板坡道上目睹了事情的全过程。"其实，倘若他们都能像米泰一样懂得那么多数学知识，你们可能会赢几场比赛。"

　　"数学？"我反问道。

　　"数学，"玛丽·贝斯说。

　　"数学！"米泰惊呼。

　　"数学？"我又一次反问道。

　　"米泰可以运用他的数学天赋来应对以后的比赛，"玛丽·贝斯继续解释道，"玩橄榄球其实就是在做数学题：角度、弧度、距离——"

　　"还有坐标两点之间的关系，"米泰补充道。尽管我听不明白，但

---

ramp　*n.* 斜坡　　　　　　　　　　　exclaim　*v.* 惊叫

arc　*n.* 弧　　　　　　　　　　　　　grid　*n.* 格子

From the gleam in his eyes I could tell Miltie knew exactly what Mary Beth was talking about, even if I didn't. "Thanks for the idea, Mary Beth," he said. "But I don't think I can do it."

"Of course you can do it!" she said, giving his hand a *squeeze*. "You're Miltie Math-head! Just let me know if I can help."

"Help!" I thought. But Mary Beth was right. Overnight, Miltie worked up a bunch of cool, new plays. The only one who would need help from us would be our competitors, if we could only get our teammates to go along with Miltie's plan.

Miltie was nervous about showing the guys his plays, so I gave him a pep talk and that gave him some self-confidence.

看着米泰眼睛放光，我知道米泰很明白玛丽·贝斯所说的话。"玛丽·贝斯，谢谢你的提醒，"他说，"但是我觉得做不到。"

"你当然能了！"她说着，用力捏了一下米泰的手说，"你可是数学天才米泰呀！需要帮助的话，随时叫我。"

"帮助！"我沉思着。玛丽·贝斯说得对。经过彻夜研究，米泰整理出了很多新奇的打法。如果我们的队员能够实施米泰的战术计划，那么唯一需要帮助的人恐怕只有我们的对手了。

米泰想到要向队友展示他研究出的新打法，感觉很紧张，所以我给他打了打气，这让他增添了不少自信。

---

squeeze *n.* 紧握

"A football field is just a big *rectangle* that is 100 yards long and 53.3 yards wide," Miltie began.

"Boring!" yelled Jimmy.

"I'm snoring!" said Beefalo.

"We know the size of the field, Milton," Jakey-boy, our tight end *chimed in*. "Just tell us the plays."

"Okay. According to my statistics, Dan here can throw a pass up to 33 yards—that's one-third of the field—about 82 percent of the time." Miltie drew on the chalkboard to explain.

"In this play, we take advantage of Dan's strong arm and Jimmy's speed. Jimmy starts on the line of *scrimmage* exactly three yards

---

"一个橄榄球场地就是一个长100码，宽53.3码的大矩形，"米泰开始了讲解。

"太无聊了！"吉米喊道。

"我都要打呼噜了，"皮弗娄牛说。

"米尔顿，我们都知道场地的大小，"小杰克——我们的近端锋插话了，"你只管告诉我们你的计划就好了。"

"好。根据我的数据分析，丹在这里传33码——即三分之一场地——大概只需要之前时间的82%。"米泰在黑板上画图来作以解释。

"用这种打法，我们可以充分利用丹强大的臂力和吉米的速度。吉米

---

rectangle *n.* 矩形　　　　　　　　　　　　　　　　chime in 插话
scrimmage *n.* 争球

to the right of Jakey-boy. They both run straight down the field, together, but not touching, like two *parallel* lines—

"Para-what?" asked Jimmy.

"Parallel," said Miltie. "Next to each other, like the lines on a piece of notebook paper."

"Or the ten-yard lines that go across the football field," added Jakey-boy.

"You'll run parallel for 20 yards, and then Jakey-boy will make a 90-degree turn to the right to cut across the perpendicular."

"Huh?"

"*Perpendicular*, Jakey-boy. At a right angle to the direction Jimmy

就在离小杰克正好3码的争球线出发。他们一起在场地里跑直线，但是不要互相接触，就像两条平行线——

"平什么？"吉米问道。

"平行线，"米泰接着说，"一个挨一个，就像笔记本里的线条一样。"

"或者在穿过球场的10码线处。"小杰克补充道。

"你们平行跑20码，然后小杰克将会有一个90度的大转弯，转向右边，垂直抄近路通过。"

"啊？"

"要垂直，小杰克。正好是吉米跑的那个角度。"

parallel *adj.* 平行的   perpendicular *adj.* 垂直的

is running," I said.

The guys murmured my name, as if I was to blame for Miltie's math lessons. But it all made sense when Miltie added lots of X's and arrows to his picture, like real pro coaches do.

"You cut straight to the sideline, right behind Jimmy, taking the attention of his defender with you. That's when Jimmy goes into overdrive and Danny lofts a pass into his *outstretched* arms."

The *grumbling* quieted down as Miltie went on to explain other plays. My favorite was called "Angles to the End Zone."

Jimmy and Jakey-boy were to line up on opposite sides of the offensive line. Each runs toward the opposite corner of the end

---

队友们嘀咕着我的名字，好像在责怪我让米泰来上这堂数学课。但随着米泰不断完善那幅图，标出了许多"X"和箭头，一切都明朗了，倒有点真正专业教练的范儿。

"你直接切直跑到边线，就在吉米正后方，分散防守他的人的注意力。吉米趁机加快速度，丹尼此时传高球，就会正中吉米怀里。"

米泰继续讲着他的战术，嘈杂声也渐渐平息下来。我最欣赏的一招是"到达阵区的角度"。

吉米和小杰克在对方防线对面排成一列。两人分别朝着对方的两端

---

outstretched *adj.* 延伸的 　　　　　　　　　　　　grumble *v.* 抱怨

zone. But at the point where they would crisscross, or *intersect*, they change direction and run to the corner of the end zone on their side of the field. The defense would be confused; I'd find the open man and throw the ball for a *touchdown*. Bam!

Football Hero

Thanks to Miltie's plays we won three games in a row and finished the season 7-3, tied with our rivals, the Mudflat Maulers. A playoff game would decide the championship.

The Maulers were led by a huge *linebacker* named Maurice, but no one dared call him that. He went by the name "618." Some guys said that was his weight, but it was short for his nickname, "The 618

达阵区跑去。但是在某一点他们可能会十字相遇，此时他们要改变方向，向各自半场的达阵区跑去。对方防守会出现混乱；我就找到无人防守的队员，然后传球给他，触地得分。砰！

橄榄球英雄

多亏米泰的战术，我们连赢三场，以7:3完结了本赛季的比赛，与对手马蒂福莱特莫乐队打成平手。一场季后赛将决定最后的冠军。

莫乐队是由一个强壮的中后卫球员毛瑞斯带队的，但是没有人敢那样称呼他。大家都叫他"618"。有人说这个数字代表他的体重，但实际上是他绰号"618高速"的简称。他要冲起锋来，就如疾驰的火车脱离轨道

intersect *v.* 交错　　　　　　　touchdown *n.* 底线得分
linebacker *n.* 后卫队员

Express." When he charged, it was like a train barreling down the tracks. Whenever he tackled the ball-carrier he shouted, "The 618 is right on time."

Fortunately, Beefalo kept 618 out of my way long enough to set Miltie's plays in *motion*. Jimmy gained twenty-five yards in one play, and then ran another twenty-five for a touchdown.

"I covered one quarter of the field on each run," Jimmy proudly said to Miltie. Jimmy's math grade had improved since Miltie started calling our plays. "Add them together, and that's half the field."

We scored again on the "Angles to the End Zone" play. Meanwhile, we held the Maulers to a field goal.

一样。任何时候他扭住持球队员时都会大喊："618来得真是时候呀。"

　　幸运的是，皮弗娄牛一直挡着618不让他挡住我，才为米泰战术的顺利实施赢得了足够的时间。吉米在一场比赛中跑出了25码，在另一场比赛中跑了25码触地得分。

　　"我每场跑的距离都有场地的四分之一。"吉米自豪地跟米泰炫耀。自从米泰开始指挥比赛后，吉米的数学能力有了一定的提高。"把所有我跑过的路程加起来估计已有半个场地了。"

　　我们利用"达阵区角度"战术又得了一分。与此同时，我们还化解了莫乐队的一个三分球。

motion *n.* 移动

At the start of the fourth quarter, we were still ahead 14-3, but they scored right away on the kick-off. Then came the big blow.

We had the ball on the Mauler 20-yard line and were set up for a field goal. It would be an easy kick for Beefalo, even with The 618 Express coming in full speed.

I took the snap. Beefalo *booted* the ball into the air. Then I heard a snap. This time, it was my wrist.

"The 618 is right on time!" cried out the Mauler as he ran right over me. "Even if it jumped the track," he laughed under his breath. The guy had *steamrolled* me on purpose.

I was out of the game. The field goal was good, which made me

---

在第四节比赛开始时，我们依然以14：3遥遥领先，但一开球他们就得分了。随之而来的是重大的打击。

我们在莫乐队20码线处控球，本来是要准备进一个三分球。尽管618正全速赶来，但对于皮弗娄牛来说，应该是不费吹灰之力的一次射门。

我用力一踢。皮弗娄牛一脚把球踢向空中。我听见啪的一声响。这一次，却是我的手腕在响。

"618来得正是时候呀。"毛瑞斯把我撞倒在地，还大声叫喊。"虽然我开小差咯"。他气喘吁吁地笑道。这家伙是故意撞到我的。

我被罚出局。好在那个三分球顺利拿下，这让我稍感欣慰，但好景

---

boot v. 猛踢

steamroll v. 粉碎

feel a little better, but not for long. The Maulers scored again to tie the game, then they kicked a field goal to go ahead 20-17.

With me out, our backup quarterback Philly Stone took over, and he was plainly nervous. He *fumbled* on his first play, but luckily Beefalo recovered the ball. Then he threw an interception on the third play. Finally, in the last minute, with Miltie calling the plays, Philly put together a drive to the Mauler 15-yard line.

It was fourth down with three seconds on the clock. A field goal would send the game to sudden-death overtime—the first team to score wins.

Miltie called a time-out. The team gathered around.

不长。莫乐队又得分了，使得我们暂时打成平局，后来他们又进了个三分球，以20:17领先。

随着我出局，后备四分卫费利·斯通接替了我的位置，他紧张得不行。他第一节就失球了，幸好皮弗娄牛救回了球。在第三节中，他传出的球又被对方拦截。在最后一分钟，随着米泰在旁指挥，费利奋力跑向莫乐队15码线处。

此时，我们的最后一次进攻只剩下三秒钟的时间了。在加时赛中，比赛规则为"突然死亡法"——即最先得分的队获胜。

米泰叫了暂停。所有队员围在了一起。

---

fumble *v.* （尤用于体育运动）失球；接球失误

"I say we kick the field goal, then get them in overtime," said Beefalo.

"What if you miss?" asked Philly.

"I won't," said Beefalo. "We're at the 15-yard line. That's only fifteen-hundredths of the field— a *cinch* for me."

"But what if I mess up?" said Philly. "You saw what 618 did to Dan. That's not helping my nerves."

He had a point.

"Forget the field goal," said Miltie. "Let's go for it." A *hush* replaced the usual *huddle hubbub*. "I've got a plan."

"A plan?" scoffed Beefalo. "Why should we let a math-head

"依我看我们射门，让他们进入加时赛。"皮弗娄牛建议道。

"如果你没有进呢？"费利反问。

"不会的，"皮弗娄牛回答说："我们现在在15码线上，也就是15/100的领域，我绝对有把握。"

"但是万一我搞砸了怎么办？"费利担心地说。"你也看到了618是怎么对丹了。想到这就让我提心吊胆。"

他倒说到点子上了。

"别想着射门了，"米泰说，"我们就放手一搏吧。"大家没有像平时那样喧哗，只是发出了一片嘘声。"我有个计划"。

"一个计划？"皮弗娄牛嘲笑道。"我们为什么要让一个数学天才决

---

cinch *n.* 有把握的事情
huddle *n.* 队员靠拢（磋商战术）

hush *n.* 静寂；嘘声
hubbub *n.* 喧闹

decide what happens to this team?"

"Because Miltie got us here with his plans," said Jimmy. "I, for one, want to know what Miltie has to say."

"Miltie, Miltie, Miltie," sang out the team.

Miltie looked around at his cheering teammates. The deer-in-the-headlights look in his eyes was gone, and in its place was a *fiery glint*.

"We set up to kick the field goal," said Miltie. "But we don't."

A trick play! That Miltie wasn't just a math genius; he had a head for football.

"Remember the old *triple reverse* that Mr. McGruder showed us?

定我们队的命运？"

"因为是米泰的战术让我们走到了现在，"吉米说，"我为自己表个态，我想听听米泰的计划。"

"米泰，米泰，米泰。"队员们大声呼喊。

米泰环视了一下欢呼的队友。他眼中呆若木鸡的神情已全然消失，一股炽热喷薄而出。

"我们装作射门，"米泰说，"实际上不射。"

使诈！米泰不仅是数学天才，还是橄榄球天才呀！

"还记得迈克格鲁德先生给我们展示过的三重逆向法吗？不要向我传

---

fiery *adj.* 火一般的

triple *n.* 三倍的

glint *n.* 闪光；闪亮

reverse *n.* 颠倒

Instead of the snap coming to me, holding the ball for the place-kicker, it goes directly to Beefalo."

"Whoa," I said. "I get the triple reverse part. But don't you mean Philly doesn't get the snap?"

"Normally, that would be the situation with you out, Dan. But I'm going in, not Philly."

Miltie Meyers at quarterback?

"You'll be right in the path of The 618 Express," said Philly.

"Exactly," said Miltie. "That's where I want to be."

"But Miltie, that runaway train must be a foot taller than you and weigh three times as much," I said. "And I can tell you from *personal* experience, you don't want to get in his way."

球，带着球给定位球员，然后直接传给皮弗娄牛。"

"哇。"我惊呼。"我明白是怎么个'三重逆向'了。但是你是说不把球传给费利了？"

"你出局的时候我们一般都用那种战术。但是这次我上场，费利不上。"

米泰·迈耶在四分卫？

"你正好站在'618高速'的道上。"费利说。

"说得对，"米泰说道。"那就是我想站的地方"

"但是米泰，那个脱缰野马要比你高出一英尺，比你重两倍呢。"我说，"以我个人经验来看，你不该挡他的道。"

---

personal *adj.* 个人的

"I wasn't planning to," he said. "In fact, my size will be to my advantage WHEN I TAKE HIM OUT."

"Miltie, Miltie, Miltie!" cheered the guys again, clapping each other on the back.

"Besides, nobody messes with my old pal, Dan-the-Man," Miltie said.

Miltie put on his helmet, which for the first time, seemed to fit just right. He led the team back onto the field and took his spot about five yards behind our center.

"Hike!" Miltie called. The ball was snapped, as planned, past Miltie to Beefalo. In came the charging 618 just as Jakey-boy came around for a *handoff*. Jimmy *swung* around from the other end for his handoff.

The rushing 618 stayed right on track, not fooled by the play.

"我也没打算挡，"他说，"事实上，我正好可以利用我的体型让他出局。"

"米泰，米泰，米泰！"队友们再次欢呼，互相拍背。

"还得让他们看看谁还敢惹我的老朋友大男人丹。"米泰说。

米泰戴上头盔——也是有史以来第一次似乎有了合适的头盔。他带领着队友回到场地，在离中线5码的地方踩好点。

"开球！"米泰叫道。球按计划快速传递，经过米泰到皮弗娄牛。在小杰克来回准备传球时，618开始冲锋了。吉米便转过身从另一侧传球。

冲锋的618并没有中计，还是在继续冲锋。米泰站起来拦截他。在人

---

handoff *n.* 传球　　　　　　　　　　　　swing *v.* 突然转身

Miltie stood up to block him. Above the roar of the crowd, I heard Mary Beth cry, "Watch out, Miltie!" Then, just as 618 about ran over Miltie to *demolish* Jimmy, Miltie dropped to his knees and *braced* himself on the ground. The 618 Express, expecting to flatten someone a few feet higher up, tripped over Miltie's backside and went flying high. When the Mauler finally landed, Jimmy and the football were safe in the end zone.

Miltie Math-head had *derailed* The 618 Express and led our team to victory. The team raised Miltie on their shoulders and carried him around the field.

"Miltie, Miltie, Miltie," they cheered.

"I knew you could do it," I said. "Football is all about math."

"Actually, Dan," he said smiling, "for this play, I used *physics* — but I'll tell you all about that later."

群的咆哮声中，我听见玛丽·贝斯呼喊："米泰，小心！"正当618想要撞倒米泰，借此推倒吉米时，米泰屈膝，撑倒在地。"618高速"本想撞飞一个人，结果绊倒在米泰的后背上，自己飞了起来。等毛瑞斯着地时，吉米和橄榄球都安全稳健地落在了达阵区。

　　数学天才米泰逐出了"618高速"，带领我们队赢得了胜利。队员们把米泰扛在肩上绕场庆祝。

　　"米泰，米泰，米泰。"他们欢呼着。

　　"我就知道你行的。"我说，"比橄榄球就是比数学。"

　　"丹，"他笑着答道，"其实最后一次进攻，我用了物理知识，至于细节我以后告诉你吧。"

---

demolish *v.* 推翻　　　　　　　　　　　　brace *v.* 支撑

derail *v.* 使……出局　　　　　　　　　　physics *n.* 物理